EXODUS

Chapters 1—18

J. Vernon McGee

THOMAS NELSON PUBLISHERS

Nashville • Atlanta • London • Vancouver

Published in Nashville, Tennessee, by Thomas Nelson, Inc.

Scripture quotations are from the KING JAMES VERSION of the Bible.

Library of Congress Cataloging-in-Publication Data

McGee, J. Vernon (John Vernon), 1904–1988
   [Thru the Bible with J. Vernon McGee]
   Thru the Bible commentary series / J. Vernon McGee.
    p.   cm.
   Reprint. Originally published: Thru the Bible with J. Vernon McGee. 1975.
   Includes bibliographical references.
   ISBN 0-7852-1004-0 (TR)
   ISBN 0-7852-1070-9 (NRM)
   1. Bible—Commentaries. I. Title.
BS491.2.M37 1991
220.7'7—dc20
                                     90–41340
                                        CIP

Printed in the United States of America

2 3 4 5 6 7 8 9 — 99 98 97 96 95

CONTENTS

EXODUS—Chapters 1—18

PREFACE

The radio broadcasts of the Thru the Bible Radio five-year program were transcribed, edited, and published first in single-volume paperbacks to accommodate the radio audience.

There has been a minimal amount of further editing for this publication. Therefore, these messages are not the word-for-word recording of the taped messages which went out over the air. The changes were necessary to accommodate a reading audience rather than a listening audience.

These are popular messages, prepared originally for a radio audience. They should not be considered a commentary on the entire Bible in any sense of that term. These messages are devoid of any attempt to present a theological or technical commentary on the Bible. Behind these messages is a great deal of research and study in order to interpret the Bible from a popular rather than from a scholarly (and too-often boring) viewpoint.

We have definitely and deliberately attempted "to put the cookies on the bottom shelf so that the kiddies could get them."

The fact that these messages have been translated into many languages for radio broadcasting and have been received with enthusiasm reveals the need for a simple teaching of the whole Bible for the masses of the world.

I am indebted to many people and to many sources for bringing this volume into existence. I should express my especial thanks to my secretary, Gertrude Cutler, who supervised the editorial work; to Dr. Elliott R. Cole, my associate, who handled all the detailed work with the publishers; and finally, to my wife Ruth for tenaciously encouraging me from the beginning to put my notes and messages into printed form.

Solomon wrote, ". . . of making many books there is no end; and much study is a weariness of the flesh" (Eccl. 12:12). On a sea of books that flood the marketplace, we launch this series of THRU THE BIBLE with the hope that it might draw many to the one Book, *The Bible*.

J. VERNON MCGEE

The Book of
EXODUS

INTRODUCTION

Exodus continues the account which was begun in Genesis, although there was a lapse of at least 3½ centuries. Genesis 15:13 says that the seed of Abraham would spend 400 years in Egypt. Exodus 12:40 says that it was 430 years, and Galatians 3:16–17 confirms it. It was 430 years from the call of Abraham, and 400 years from the time that God told Abraham.

Exodus means "the way out" and tells the story of redemption by blood and by power. The message of Exodus is stated in Hebrews 11:23–29, which says: "By faith Moses, when he was born, was hid three months of his parents, because they saw he was a proper child; and they were not afraid of the king's commandment. By faith Moses, when he was come to years, refused to be called the son of Pharaoh's daughter; choosing rather to suffer affliction with the people of God, than to enjoy the pleasures of sin for a season; esteeming the reproach of Christ greater riches than the treasures in Egypt: for he had respect unto the recompence of the reward. By faith he forsook Egypt, not fearing the wrath of the king: for he endured, as seeing him who is invisible. Through faith he kept the passover, and the sprinkling of blood, lest he that destroyed the firstborn should touch them. By faith they passed through the Red sea as by dry land: which the Egyptians assaying to do were drowned."

The word which opens Exodus is a conjunction that is better translated *and* rather than *now*. Exodus has been called the sequel to Genesis. Dr. G. Campbell Morgan wrote, "In the Book of Exodus nothing is commenced, nothing is finished."

Genesis 46:27 tells us that seventy souls of Jacob entered Egypt. It is conservatively estimated that 2,100,000 left Egypt at the time of the Exodus. Although it is impossible to be certain about dates in this early period, it would seem that Joseph entered Egypt under the Hyksos or shepherd kings who were Semitic conquerors, and were related to Abraham, Isaac, and Jacob. Actually the Israelites may have been their only friends, as they were hated by Egyptians. Finally they were driven out by a native Egyptian dynasty which was understandably hostile to foreigners. In this line was the Pharaoh of the oppression and the one "who knew not Joseph."

Moses figures prominently in the Book of Exodus. He is the author of the Pentateuch which includes the first five books of the Old Testament—Genesis, Exodus, Leviticus, Numbers, and Deuteronomy. In the Book of Exodus, Moses' life is divided into three forty-year periods:

1. Forty years in Pharaoh's palace in Egypt
2. Forty years in the desert in Midian
3. Forty years in the wilderness as leader of Israel

Moses' training in Egypt, evidently in the Temple of the Sun, did not prepare him to follow God in leading Israel out of Egypt. God trained him in the desert for forty years to reveal to him that he could not deliver Israel alone. God gave Moses a B.D. (Backside of the Desert) degree.

It should be noted that after God prepared Moses to deliver his people, He sent him back to Egypt after forty years. Moses is to assemble elders of Israel and go to Pharaoh. Pharaoh will refuse to let Israel go. His refusal will open the contest between God and the gods of Egypt. Egypt was dominated by idolatry—"gods many and lords many." There were thousands of temples and millions of idols. Behind idolatry was Satan. There was power in the religion of Egypt—"Now as Jannes and Jambres withstood Moses, so do these also resist the truth: men of corrupt minds, reprobate concerning the faith" (2 Tim. 3:8). Pharaoh asked, ". . . Who is the LORD, that I should obey his voice to let Israel go? I know not the LORD, neither will I let Israel go" (Exod. 5:2). God introduced Himself. Pharaoh got acquainted with God and acknowledged Him as God. "And Pharaoh sent, and called for Moses and Aaron, and said unto them, I have sinned this time: the LORD is righteous, and I and my people are wicked" (Exod. 9:27). "Then Pharaoh called for Moses and Aaron in haste; and he said, I have sinned against the LORD your God, and against you" (Exod. 10:16).

A question arises from this episode: Why the plagues? They were God's battle with the gods of Egypt. Each plague was directed against a particular god in Egypt. "For I will pass through the land of Egypt this night, and will smite all the firstborn in the land of Egypt, both man and beast; and against all the gods of Egypt I will execute judgment: I am the LORD" (Exod. 12:12). God wanted to reveal to His own people that He, the LORD, was far greater than any god of Egypt and that He had power to deliver them.

OUTLINE

I. **A Deliverer, Chapters 1—11**
   A. Slavery of Israel in Egypt, Chapter 1
   B. Birth of Moses—First Forty Years in Pharaoh's Palace, Chapter 2
   C. Call of Moses—Second Forty Years in Midian, Chapter 3
      (*Incident of burning bush*)
   D. Return of Moses to Egypt—Announcement of Deliverance to Israel, Chapter 4
   E. Contest with Pharaoh, Chapters 5—11
      (*9 plagues against idolatry of Egypt, battle of the gods*)

II. **Deliverance (by Blood and Power), Chapters 12—14**
   A. Institution of Passover—Tenth Plague, Death of Firstborn (Blood), Chapter 12
   B. Crossing Red Sea—Destruction of Army of Egypt (Power), Chapters 13—14

III. **Marching to Mount Sinai (Spiritual Education), Chapters 15—18**
   (*7 experiences correspond to Christian experience*)
   A. Song of Redeemed—Wilderness of Shur, Chapter 15:1–22
      (*No bed of roses after redemption*)
   B. Marah, Bitter Water Sweetened by Tree, Chapter 15:23–26
      (*Cross sweetens bitter experiences of life*)
   C. Elim (Fruitful Christian Experience), Chapter 15:27
   D. Wilderness of Sin—Manna and Quail, Chapter 16
      (*Christ is the Bread of Life.*)
   E. Smitten Rock ("That Rock was Christ"), Chapter 17:1–7
   F. Amalek (the Flesh), Chapter 17:8–16
      (*Victory on the hill top, Deut. 25:17–18*)
   G. Jethro, Priest of Midian, Chapter 18
      (*Worldly wisdom in contrast to revelation*)

CHAPTER 1

THEME: Israel in Egypt; the heroism of two women

The first few verses of Exodus connect it with the account of Genesis. Those who came down into Egypt are listed first and the years between are quickly covered. Exodus 1:7 continues the Genesis account.

The key verse in this book is Exodus 20:2, which says, "I am the LORD thy God, which have brought thee out of the land of Egypt, out of the house of bondage."

ISRAEL IN EGYPT

Now these are the names of the children of Israel, which came into Egypt; every man and his household came with Jacob.

Reuben, Simeon, Levi, and Judah,

Issachar, Zebulun, and Benjamin,

Dan, and Naphtali, Gad, and Asher.

And all the souls that came out of the loins of Jacob were seventy souls: for Joseph was in Egypt already.

And Joseph died, and all his brethren, and all that generation [Exod. 1:1–6].

Exodus is the sequel to Genesis. The death of Joseph concludes Genesis. Exodus 1:6 tells us that Joseph, all of his brethren, and all that generation had died. Three and one-half centuries have passed.

In Genesis chapter 46 God said that Israel would increase and multiply and become a great nation in the land of Egypt. As we come to verse seven, this prophecy has actually taken place.

> **And the children of Israel were fruitful, and increased abundantly, and multiplied, and waxed exceeding mighty; and the land was filled with them [Exod. 1:7].**

Verse eight indicates that a great change has taken place.

> **Now there arose up a new king over Egypt, which knew not Joseph [Exod. 1:8].**

A new Pharaoh has come to the throne of Egypt who has never heard of Joseph. Perhaps the Hyksos or shepherd kings, who were Semites, had been deposed and the former dynasty of Egyptian kings sat on the throne again. The new king never knew Joseph and felt no indebtedness to him or his descendants.

There is a tremendous lesson to be learned in verse eight. I have often wondered why movements today which specialize in reaching children have not used this verse. It should be used. There is a continual responsiblity of teaching the Word of God to each generation. If we neglect to teach the Bible, the time will come when it will be forgotten.

A Coca-Cola executive in Texas once told me that a certain percentage of each bottle is spent for advertising. I kidded him about having to advertise such a well-known product. I mentioned to this man that I had once seen thirteen Coca-Cola advertisements in a small town in Texas and thought that was overdoing it. He said, "Not so!" Then he asked me, "When was the last time you saw a can of Arbuckle coffee?" I told him that it had been a popular brand when I was a boy, but I had not seen any lately. "They thought," he replied, "that they did not need to advertise."

Now there arose in Egypt a Pharaoh that did not know Joseph. And there is always a new generation that has never heard about the Lord Jesus Christ. I was shocked not long ago when I realized my own daughter and son-in-law had no knowledge of the Depression. They are of a new generation that did not live through the Depression. They did not understand what some of us older folk went through in the way of hardship and suffering. Therefore it is always necessary to teach the next generation what happened in previous generations. And so there arose a generation who never heard of Joseph. At one time Joseph was so well known that he was a hero and his body could not even be taken from the land.

The new Pharaoh who came to power was not as kindly disposed toward the Israelites as had been his predecessors.

> **And he said unto his people, Behold, the people of the children of Israel are more and mightier than we:**
>
> **Come on, let us deal wisely with them; lest they multiply, and it come to pass, that, when there falleth out any war, they join also unto our enemies, and fight against us, and so get them up out of the land [Exod. 1:9–10].**

It was a real possibility that Israel might have joined forces with the enemy against Egypt.

Although Pharaoh wanted slaves, the simple way to solve the problem would have been to let Israel go. Instead of releasing Israel, Pharaoh decided to use worldly wisdom to take care of the difficulty.

> **Therefore they did set over them taskmasters to afflict them with their burdens. And they built for Pharaoh treasure cities, Pithom and Raamses [Exod. 1:11].**

The children of Israel were forced to do hard labor. They did not build the pyramids because they had already been in existence many, many years. They were, however, forced to build treasure cities. They built the treasure cities of Pithom and Raamses. They constructed the cities with bricks which they as slaves were forced to make. At the beginning of their slavery the Israelites were provided with straw to make their bricks. As Pharaoh's persecution of them increased, they were compelled to hunt for their own straw and at the same time produce the exact number of bricks they had made before. Dr. Kyle, one of my professors, brought a brick to class one day that had been taken out of the city of Raamses. The brick was made without straw. The biblical record of Israel's bondage in Egypt needs no defense; the brick only confirms that the record is accurate.

There is no doubt that the Israelites were in a difficult position in Egypt. The Egyptians made life harder and harder for Israel.

> **But the more they afflicted them, the more they multiplied and grew. And they were grieved because of the children of Israel [Exod. 1:12].**

God told Abraham that Israel would have times of hardship in Egypt. Genesis 15:13 says, "And he said unto Abram, Know of a surety that thy seed shall be a stranger in a land that is not theirs, and shall serve them; and they shall afflict them four hundred years." Three things are predicted in this verse. The Israelites were to be strangers in a strange land; they were to be servants, that is, slaves; they were to be afflicted. All of these predictions had come true in just the first few verses of Exodus 1.

The more the Egyptians afflicted the Israelites, the more they multiplied and grew.

> **And the Egyptians made the children of Israel to serve with rigour:**
>
> **And they made their lives bitter with hard bondage, in mortar, and in brick, and in all manner of service in the field: all their service, wherein they made them serve, was with rigour.**
>
> **And the king of Egypt spake to the Hebrew midwives, of which the name of the one was Shiphrah, and the name of the other Puah [Exod. 1:13–15].**

The Egyptians not only made slaves of the Israelites, they mistreated them also. In spite of the persecution, God's blessing rested upon them and their numbers increased greatly. The king noticed the rapid growth of his slave nation and spoke to the Hebrew midwives in an attempt to solve the problem.

It is interesting to note the meaning of the names of these two women. Shiphrah means "beauty." Puah means "splendor." Have you ever noticed the silhouette pictures of Egyptian women? Beauty and splendor characterized the women in the land of Egypt. These women apparently occupied high official positions in Egypt and were in charge of the nurses who were responsible for delivering babies.

> And he said, When ye do the office of a midwife to the Hebrew women, and see them upon the stools; if it be a son, then ye shall kill him: but if it be a daughter, then she shall live [Exod. 1:16].

This is another attempt of Satan to destroy the line leading to the Lord Jesus Christ. Satanic attempts to cut off the line leading to Christ run all the way through the Bible from the Old Testament to the New Testament. Many attempts have been made to destroy the Jews, and it is quite interesting to note the way anti-Semitism has spread throughout the world. It is satanic in its origin, and therefore no child of God should have any part in it. It is generally people with no knowledge of God who persecute the Jews.

Someone is undoubtedly thinking, "Yes, but during the Dark Ages, the church engaged in anti-Semitism." This is true. But it was the Dark Ages and the church was far from the Word of God, involved in external religious affairs. In my opinion no person can study the Word of God and become anti-Semitic.

THE HEROISM OF TWO WOMEN

As Satan attempted to get rid of the children of Israel, God intervened.

> But the midwives feared God, and did not as the king of Egypt commanded them, but saved the men children alive.

> And the king of Egypt called for the midwives, and said unto them, Why have ye done this thing, and have saved the men children alive?

And the midwives said unto Pharaoh, Because the Hebrew women are not as the Egyptian women; for they are lively, and are delivered ere the midwives come in unto them.

Therefore God dealt well with the midwives: and the people multiplied, and waxed very mighty [Exod. 1:17-20].

This attempt to destroy all the male Hebrew children was a political maneuver that did not work out.

And it came to pass, because the midwives feared God, that he made them houses [Exod. 1:21].

These women had to choose whether to obey Pharaoh or God. They had learned to fear God and their obedience was seen and rewarded by God. He gave Shiphrah and Puah both a name and a place in Israel, and they were greatly respected in the land.

And Pharaoh charged all his people, saying, Every son that is born ye shall cast into the river, and every daughter ye shall save alive [Exod. 1:22].

If this order had been carried out, Israel would soon have been exterminated. Pharaoh's orders were not obeyed, and the succeeding chapters in Exodus clearly show it. God raises up Moses to deliver the children of Israel out of Egyptian bondage. Exodus is the great book on redemption. It reveals, in picture form, how God delivers us today—from sin, the world, the flesh, and the Devil—and saves us for heaven.

CHAPTER 2

THEME: The birth of Moses; Moses' first attempt to help his people; Moses in Midian takes a gentile bride

In this chapter we have before us Moses the deliverer. He is prominent as the deliverer of Israel in the first eleven chapters of Exodus.

Exodus is the great book of redemption. Nothing is begun or ended in this book. It is simply a continuation of the story that started in Genesis and continues on into the Books of Leviticus and Numbers.

THE BIRTH OF MOSES

And there went a man of the house of Levi, and took to wife a daughter of Levi.

And the woman conceived, and bare a son: and when she saw him that he was a goodly child, she hid him three months [Exod. 2:1–2].

This is the age-old story of the man who sees a woman, falls in love with her, and marries her. She loves him in return, and they have a child. This is what human life is all about, and that is the story we have here.

Moses is writing this account of his parents and of his own birth, and it is a modest record. This is why we must turn to other portions of the Bible to give us more information about the events in Exodus. If given the opportunity, most of us would want to tell about our parents in detail, but Moses did not even mention his parents by name. They were ordinary people. They were in slavery. They were members of the tribe of Levi. That is all Moses says at this point. Later on we are given their names as Amram and Jochebed.

Verse two tells us only that Moses was a good, healthy child.

Moses also seems quite reticent about giving his own record in any
detail.

> **And when she could not longer hide him, she took for
> him an ark of bulrushes, and daubed it with slime and
> with pitch, and put the child therein; and she laid it in
> the flags by the river's brink [Exod. 2:3].**

Moses was not only a healthy child, but he also had a good set of
lungs. His parents could hide him at first, but the day came when
Moses could really scream at the top of his voice. What a contrast this
is to several years later when the Lord asks him to be His spokesman to
Pharaoh and Moses says that he cannot speak. Many of us are good at
crying like babies, but as adults we do not do so well for the Lord.

Jochebed had a serious problem. She could no longer hide her
child. A lot of pious people would have acted differently from this
mother by saying, "Well, we're just going to trust the Lord." That is a
wonderful statement to make, but do you really trust the Lord when
you are playing the fool? Jochebed would have been foolish to keep
her child in the house when a guard passing by might have heard his
cry. It would have meant instant death for Moses.

I can hear someone saying, "You know the child would not cry
when the guard passed by." How do you know? Faith is *not* a leap in
the dark, as I heard a liberal say some years ago. God asks us to believe
that which is good and solid. God never asks us to do foolish things.
Jochebed did a sensible thing. She made a little ark and put Moses
in it.

> **And his sister stood afar off, to wit what would be done
> to him [Exod. 2:4].**

In addition to fashioning the ark, Jochebed also sent Moses' sister to
watch it and find out what would happen to her brother. Her sensible
actions indicated that she was trusting God.

> **And the daughter of Pharaoh came down to wash herself
> at the river; and her maidens walked along by the river's**

**side; and when she saw the ark among the flags, she
sent her maid to fetch it [Exod. 2:5].**

Now the hand of the Lord is revealed. The Lord is going to intervene in
this situation. This is what the Lord does when you use common
sense, and Jochebed had demonstrated sensibleness. Pharaoh's
daughter came to the Nile River to wash. It was undoubtedly a se-
cluded spot. And there was an ark. She had one of her attendants
bring the ark to her.

**And when she had opened it, she saw the child: and,
behold, the babe wept. And she had compassion on him,
and said, This is one of the Hebrews' children [Exod.
2:6].**

At that very moment was the right time for the child to cry. In fact, the
Lord pinched little Moses and he let out a yelp. And God brought
together two things that He has made—a baby's cry and a woman's
heart. Pharaoh's daughter just could not pass this little baby by.

**Then said his sister to Pharaoh's daughter, Shall I go
and call to thee a nurse of the Hebrew women, that she
may nurse the child for thee? [Exod. 2:7].**

Miriam, Moses' sister, made a very helpful suggestion to the prin-
cess. And later on she is not going to let her young brother forget it.
This is a very human story we are reading, friends. God has something to tell us on every page of His Book.

**And Pharaoh's daughter said to her, Go. And the maid
went and called the child's mother [Exod. 2:8].**

This is a real turn of events, and it shows how God really moves when
we act sensibly and move by faith sensibly. The very mother of the
child was called to nurse him and be *paid* for it! You cannot beat that,
friends. You cannot beat God when He is moving in our hearts and
lives.

> And Pharaoh's daughter said unto her, Take this child away, and nurse it for me, and I will give thee thy wages. And the woman took the child, and nursed it.
>
> And the child grew, and she brought him unto Pharaoh's daughter, and he became her son. And she called his name Moses: and she said, Because I drew him out of the water [Exod. 2:9–10].

The name *Moses* means "drawer out" and Pharaoh's daughter named him this because she had him drawn out of the water. Although the identification of the Pharaoh of the oppression is a controversial subject and a matter of speculation, Pharaoh's daughter may have been the oldest daughter of Rameses II, or she may have been his sister. According to the Egyptian customs of the day, her firstborn son had the right to the throne. Moses would have been the next Pharaoh had Rameses II and his queen remained childless.

MOSES' FIRST ATTEMPT TO HELP HIS PEOPLE

The first forty years of Moses' life were spent in the courts of Pharaoh. He was raised and trained like an Egyptian. He looked like an Egyptian, talked like an Egyptian, and acted like an Egyptian. He was recognized as an Egyptian when he went to Midian, as we shall see later in the Book of Exodus.

Moses was educated in the great Temple of the Sun which was the outstanding university of the day. We underrate what the Egyptians knew and accomplished. Their knowledge of astronomy was phenomenal. They knew the exact distance to the sun. They worked on the theory that the earth was round and not flat. They knew a great deal about chemistry which is evidenced by the way they were able to embalm the dead. We have no process to equal it today. Their workmanship and ability with colors were fantastic. Their colors are brighter than any we have today. I am confident that our paint companies would give anything if they knew the formulas used for color by the Egyptians. They are bright, beautiful, and startling after four thousand years. (I have to paint my house about every four years!)

In addition to all of their other accomplishments, the Egyptians also had a tremendous library. And Moses, we are told, was learned in all the wisdom of the Egyptians. The one great lack in Moses' education was that he was not taught how to serve God. But do not underestimate Moses; he was an outstanding man. Stephen, in the Book of Acts, gives us some insight into this period of Moses' life: "In which time Moses was born, and was exceeding fair, and nourished up in his father's house three months: And when he was cast out, Pharaoh's daughter took him up, and nourished him for her own son. And Moses was learned in all the wisdom of the Egyptians, and was mighty in words and in deeds. And when he was full forty years old, it came into his heart to visit his brethren the children of Israel. And seeing one of them suffer wrong, he defended him, and avenged him that was oppressed, and smote the Egyptian: For he supposed his brethren would have understood how that God by his hand would deliver them: but they understood not. And the next day he shewed himself unto them as they strove, and would have set them at one again, saying, Sirs, ye are brethren; why do ye wrong one to another? But he that did his neighbour wrong thrust him away, saying, Who made thee a ruler and a judge over us? Wilt thou kill me, as thou diddest the Egyptian yesterday? Then fled Moses at this saying . . ." (Acts 7:20–29).

In other words, all of his training in Egypt did not prepare Moses to deliver the children of Israel. One day when he was out he saw one of his brethren being persecuted and beaten by one of the slave drivers, and Moses killed the guard. Moses looked around him to see if his deed had been seen—but, he did not look up. He should have looked up to God who would have forbidden him to do a thing like this because Moses is forty years ahead of God in delivering the children of Israel. Therefore God is going to put him out on the back side of the desert.

Now when Pharaoh heard this thing, he sought to slay Moses. But Moses fled from the face of Pharaoh, and dwelt in the land of Midian: and he sat down by a well [Exod. 2:15].

MOSES IN MIDIAN TAKES A GENTILE BRIDE

Moses had spent forty years in Egypt but it did not prepare him for what was to come.

> Now the priest of Midian had seven daughters: and they came and drew water, and filled the troughs to water their father's flock.
>
> And the shepherds came and drove them away: but Moses stood up and helped them, and watered their flock.
>
> And when they came to Reuel their father, he said, How is it that ye are come so soon today?
>
> And they said, An Egyptian delivered us out of the hand of the shepherds, and also drew water enough for us, and watered the flock.
>
> And he said unto his daughters, And where is he? why is it that ye have left the man? call him, that he may eat bread.
>
> And Moses was content to dwell with the man: and he gave Moses Zipporah his daughter [Exod. 2:16–21].

Zipporah is given to Moses, and he takes a bride. It is interesting that many of the men in the Old Testament are figures of Christ. Although not all details of their lives typify Christ—they couldn't—they certainly picture Christ in some way. Moses was a murderer in sharp contrast to Christ our Savior. However, Moses was a type of Christ in that he was God's chosen deliverer; he was rejected by Israel and turned to the Gentiles, taking a gentile bride; afterward he again appears as Israel's deliverer and is accepted.

And so we find Moses in the land of Midian. For the next forty years it will be his home. Two sons are born to him. In the desert he will begin his preparation to be the deliverer of Israel from their Egyptian bondage. There has always been a question relative to Moses' marital state. I am sure he must have loved his wife, but the record we have does not reveal a wonderful relationship. This part of his life is one of the things that Moses more or less passes over. The name Zipporah means "sparrow" which may indicate a small, nervous person.

> **And she bare him a son, and he called his name Gershom: for he said, I have been a stranger in a strange land.**
>
> **And it came to pass in process of time, that the king of Egypt died: and the children of Israel sighed by reason of the bondage, and they cried, and their cry came up unto God by reason of the bondage.**
>
> **And God heard their groaning, and God remembered his covenant with Abraham, with Isaac, and with Jacob.**
>
> **And God looked upon the children of Israel, and God had respect unto them [Exod. 2:22–25].**

God is getting ready to deliver the children of Israel. Moses has been trained to be that deliverer. God did not choose to deliver the Israelites because they were superior to the Egyptians, or because they had been true and faithful to Him, or because they had not gone into idolatry. These people had been most unfaithful to God. They served idols rather than Him. You will recall that, after they had been delivered from Egypt and Moses had led them into the wilderness, the Israelites could not wait to make a golden calf to worship. God's desire was to deliver them because they were in a helpless, hopeless position in slavery. Unless someone intervened in their behalf, they would have perished.

God gives two reasons for delivering Israel:
1. He heard their groanings.
2. He remembered His covenant with Abraham, Isaac, and Jacob.

The desperate, hopeless condition of Israel appealed to the heart of God. And His promise to bring Abraham's offspring back into the land after 400 years caused God to devise a plan to deliver them.

Why do you think God has redeemed you (that is, if you are redeemed)? God saved us for the same reason He saved Israel. He found nothing in us that called for His salvation. He makes it quite clear that we are not saved because of any merit we possess. Paul explains it in Romans 3:23–24, "For all have sinned, and come short of the glory of God; being justified freely by his grace through the redemption that is in Christ Jesus." The word *freely* means "without a cause." We have been saved from our sins without a cause. It is the same word our Lord used when He said that He was hated without a cause (John 15:25). God did not look at me and say, "My, you are white and Protestant, honest and hardworking, and I'm going to redeem you." The fact of the matter is that God saw us in the blackness and darkness of sin and ignorance. He saw that we were hopelessly lost and not able to save ourselves.

God's love provided a Savior. God so loved us that He gave His only begotten Son, John 3:16 tells us. However, it was not His love that saved us; it was His *grace*. We are saved without a cause by His grace through the redemption that is in Christ Jesus.

Many people believe God saw something in them worthy of salvation. They believe God saved them as sinners, but it was because He saw what lovely people they would become. May I say that this idea is entirely erroneous. We will never become lovely. Each of us has the old nature in which no good dwells. In Romans 7:18 Paul says, "For I know that in me (that is, in my flesh,) dwelleth no good thing . . ." It is a shoe that really pinches to be told that there is no good in man at all. There never has been and never will be anything good in us. This is why we cannot produce anything good. This is why God gives us a new nature when we are saved, and why the old nature eventually must be destroyed.

God saw no good in Israel. But He heard Israel's cry in bondage and redeemed them. God saw our desperate condition and saved us. God had a plan, but He did not ask the human race what they thought about it. God did not say, "This is my plan for your salvation. If it pleases you, I will go through with it." No sir! God the Father so loved the world that He sent His Son to die for the sins of the world. The Son agreed to come, and the Father agreed to save anyone who trusted Jesus Christ for salvation. God says to us, "This is the salvation I offer you. Take it or leave it." He wants us to take it but leaves the choice up to each individual.

There was a little Scottish lady who worked hard taking in washing in order to send her son to the university. When he came home for vacation, his mind was filled with doubts about God from the liberal teaching he had received. He did not want his mother to know about the change in his thinking. She kept telling him how wonderful it was of God to save her and how she knew she was saved. Finally he could not listen to more of her talk and said, "Mother, you do not seem to realize how small you are in this universe. If you lost your soul, God would not miss it at all. It would not amount to anything." She did not reply right away but kept putting dinner on the table. Finally she said, "I've been thinking about what you said. You are right. My little soul does not amount to much; I would not lose much and God would not lose much. But if He does not save me, He will lose more than I will. He promised that if I would trust Jesus He would save me. If He breaks His word, He will lose His reputation and mar His character."

This is what God is saying to mankind. There was nothing attractive about the children of Israel but He heard their cry. There is nothing lovely about us either that would cause Him to save us. God made a covenant with Abraham, Isaac, and Jacob that promised the redemption of Israel. He also agreed to save anyone that trusts Jesus Christ as Savior. Grace is love in action. He saves us by His grace, and His great love has provided redemption.

CHAPTER 3

Moses' forty years in Midian have come to an end. All of his
schooling in Egypt was not enough to prepare him for his great
work of delivering Israel from bondage. God equipped him for this
task by forty years of preparation in the desert area of Midian.

THE CALL OF MOSES

**Now Moses kept the flock of Jethro his father in law, the
priest of Midian: and he led the flock to the backside of
the desert, and came to the mountain of God, even to
Horeb.**

**And the angel of the LORD appeared unto him in a flame
of fire out of the midst of a bush: and he looked, and,
behold, the bush burned with fire, and the bush was not
consumed [Exod. 3:1–2].**

Moses turned aside to see why the bush was burning but was not
consumed. One of the greatest proofs of the accuracy of Scripture is
the existence of the nation Israel. Years ago an emperor of Germany
asked his chaplain the question, "What is the greatest proof that the
Bible is the Word of God? That proof is somewhere in my kingdom."
Without hesitation the chaplain said, "The Jew, sir. He is the proof." He
is the burning bush that ought to cause the unbeliever to turn aside
and take a look today. It is amazing that he has existed down through
the centuries. From the days of Moses to the present hour he has been
in existence. Other nations have come and gone, and he has attended
the funeral of all of them. He is still around. Israel has been in the fire
of persecution from the bondage in Egypt through the centuries to the
present hour. But like the burning bush Israel has not been consumed.

By the way, when is the last time you saw a Midianite? Have you seen the flag of Midian? Do you know anything about the government of Midian? You do not and I do not because Midian is gone. It has disappeared.

The angel of the Lord who appeared to Moses is none other than the pre-incarnate Christ. Some people would debate this conclusion, but this is my conviction after years of studying the Word of God.

> **And Moses said, I will now turn aside, and see this great sight, why the bush is not burnt.**
>
> **And when the LORD saw that he turned aside to see, God called unto him out of the midst of the bush, and said, Moses, Moses. And he said, Here am I.**
>
> **And he said, Draw not nigh hither: put off thy shoes from off thy feet, for the place whereon thou standest is holy ground [Exod. 3:3–5]**

God had to correct Moses' manners. Although Moses had been brought up in the court of Pharaoh, he didn't know enough to take off his shoes in the presence of a holy God. And I'm afraid many folk today get familiar with God. God is teaching him a great lesson about the holiness of God. We need to learn this lesson too.

> **Moreover he said, I am the God of thy father, the God of Abraham, the God of Isaac, and the God of Jacob. And Moses hid his face; for he was afraid to look upon God [Exod. 3:6].**

Moses did not look upon God. If he had, he would have looked upon the revelation of God, the Lord Jesus Christ veiled in human form. It can still be said, "No man hath seen God at any time; the only begotten Son, which is in the bosom of the Father, he hath declared him" (John 1:18). The only way you can know God is through the Lord Jesus Christ.

And the LORD said, I have surely seen the affliction of
my people which are in Egypt, and have heard their cry
by reason of their taskmasters; for I know their sorrows;

And I am come down to deliver them out of the hand of
the Egyptians, and to bring them up out of that land
unto a good land and large, unto a land flowing with
milk and honey; unto the place of the Canaanites, and
the Hittities, and the Amorites, and the Perizzites, and
the Hivites, and the Jebusites [Exod. 3:7–8].

When God redeems, He not only redeems *from* something, He always
redeems *unto* something. We have been saved from sin unto holiness
and heaven. Paul explains this concept in Ephesians 2:5–6: "Even
when we were dead in sins, [God] hath quickened us together with
Christ, (by grace ye are saved;) and hath raised us up together, and
made us sit together in heavenly places in Christ Jesus." God has
raised us up and given us a position in Christ. If you are saved today,
you are completely saved. You will be just as saved a million years
from now as you are today because you are in Christ. You have been
brought out of Adam and put in Christ. You have been brought out of
death and put into life. You have been brought out of darkness and put
into light. You have been brought out of hell, if you please, and put
into heaven. That is *redemption:* it is *out of* and *into.*

God said, "I am going to take the children of Israel out of bondage
and into a good land." That is the salvation of God. That is redemption.

Now therefore, behold, the cry of the children of Israel is
come unto me: and I have also seen the oppression
wherewith the Egyptians oppress them.

Come now therefore, and I will send thee unto Pharaoh,
that thou mayest bring forth my people the children of
Israel out of Egypt.

> And Moses said unto God, Who am I, that I should go
> unto Pharaoh, and that I should bring forth the children
> of Israel out of Egypt? [Exod. 3:9–11].

Do you notice what has happened to Moses? Forty years before this moment, he was ready to deliver Israel. He was cocky and almost arrogant. He slew an Egyptian and delivered one of his brethren from persecution because he thought his act would be understood. He thought he could deliver Israel by himself. He found that he could not, and God took him to the back side of the desert for special training that would fit him for the job. He learned how really weak he was. He learned he could not deliver Israel by himself.

Now Moses is saying to God, "Who am I? I cannot do what you are asking me to do." My friends, *now* God can use him. This is God's way of training all of His men. God had to take the boy David who could slay a giant and put him out into the caves and dens of the earth where he was hunted like a partridge. He found out how weak he was. Then God could make him a king.

Elijah the prophet was brave enough to walk right into the court of Ahab and Jezebel and tell them that ". . . there shall not be dew nor rain these years, but according to my word" (1 Kings 17:1). Elijah was not as brave as he seemed. God put him out in the desert where He trains His men. Elijah drank from a brook. There was a drought that caused the brook to dry up. He watched the brook grow smaller and smaller and said, "My life is no more than a dried up brook." He was right. Then Elijah spent some more time eating out of an empty flour barrel. He found out he was nothing and God was everything. When Elijah realized this, God used him to face the prophets of Baal and bring down fire from heaven.

Paul puts it this way, "Therefore I take pleasure in infirmities, in reproaches, in necessities, in persecutions, in distresses for Christ's sake: for when I am weak, then am I strong" (2 Cor. 12:10). This certainly is a paradox. It is, however, what God was teaching Moses. When Moses learned that he could not deliver Israel, but that God could do it through him, God was ready to use him.

One of the reasons many of us are not used of God today is we are too strong. Have you ever stopped to think about that? God cannot use us when we are too strong. It is out of weakness that we are made strong. The apostle Paul said, "But God hath chosen the foolish things of the world to confound the wise; and God hath chosen the weak things of the world to confound the things which are mighty" (1 Cor. 1:27). Moses and Paul recognized that God could move through them when they were weak. It is amazing what God can do through a weak vessel.

And he said, Certainly, I will be with thee; and this shall be a token unto thee, that I have sent thee: When thou hast brought forth the people out of Egypt, ye shall serve God upon this mountain.

And Moses said unto God, Behold, when I come unto the children of Israel, and shall say unto them, The God of your fathers hath sent me unto you; and they shall say to me, What is his name? what shall I say unto them? [Exod. 3:12-13].

This question Moses asked is a natural one. I am sure all of us would have asked the same question. Moses was afraid that the children of Israel would not accept him. He did not know how to explain God to them. He did not know how he was ever going to get the Israelites to this mountain of God. These were the problems Moses faced. Notice how God answered him.

And God said unto Moses, I AM THAT I AM: and he said, Thus shalt thou say unto the children of Israel, I AM hath sent me unto you [Exod. 3:14].

There is undoubtedly more included in the name "I AM" than has ever been brought out, but there are several things of primary importance that should be considered. The name "I AM" is a tetragram, or a word of four letters. We translate it JEHOVAH. It has also been translated as YAHWEH. How do you pronounce it? It became a sacred name, a holy name, to the children of Israel to such an extent they actually forgot how to pronounce it. To avoid profaning His name, they did not use it. Which name, then, is correct? Is it Jehovah or Yahweh? No one knows. But "I AM" is God's name.

In Genesis God is Creator. He is Elohim, the mighty God, the self-existing One; I AM WHO I AM. This is the God who is sending Moses to deliver the children of Israel.

Psalm 135:13 says, "Thy name, O LORD, endureth for ever; and thy memorial, O LORD, throughout all generations." The name "LORD" in this verse can be translated "I AM WHO I AM." It is important to see that this name speaks of the fact that *GOD IS*.

THE COMMISSIONING OF MOSES

The time had come for the fulfillment of Joseph's promise as stated in Genesis 50:25: ". . . God will surely visit. . . ."

> **And God said moreover unto Moses, Thus shalt thou say unto the children of Israel, The LORD God of your fathers, the God of Abraham, the God of Isaac, and the God of Jacob, hath sent me unto you: this is my name for ever, and this is my memorial unto all generations [Exod. 3:15].**

God had appeared to Abraham, Isaac, and Jacob. This same God was sending Moses to the children of Israel, and the procedure he was to employ is given in the next few verses.

> **Go, and gather the elders of Israel together, and say unto them, The LORD God of your fathers, the God of Abraham, of Isaac, and of Jacob, appeared unto me, saying, I have surely visited you, and seen that which is done to you in Egypt:**

> **And I have said, I will bring you up out of the affliction of Egypt unto the land of the Canaanites, and the Hit-**

tites, and the Amorites, and the Perizzites, and the Hivites, and the Jebusites, unto a land flowing with milk and honey.

And they shall hearken to thy voice: and thou shalt come, thou and the elders of Israel, unto the king of Egypt, and ye shall say unto him, The LORD God of the Hebrews hath met with us: and now let us go, we beseech thee, three days' journey into the wilderness, that we may sacrifice to the LORD our God.

And I am sure that the king of Egypt will not let you go, no, not by a mighty hand.

And I will stretch out my hand, and smite Egypt with all my wonders which I will do in the midst thereof: and after that he will let you go [Exod. 3:16–20].

God has given Moses the agenda and course to follow. He is to tell the elders of Israel about God's plan of deliverance. Then he and the elders are to go to Pharaoh and ask to be allowed to journey three days into the wilderness to sacrifice to their God as a nation. The intention was to break gently Israel's plan to Pharaoh rather than bluntly stating, "We are leaving and going back to the land of Canaan for good."

God tells Moses that Pharaoh will refuse to let Israel go. Pharaoh's refusal in this matter will open up God's campaign against the gods of Egypt. After that campaign, even though God will show His mighty wonders, Pharaoh will still steadfastly refuse to let Israel go. God will then bring plagues that will cause Pharaoh to change his mind and send Israel on its way from Egypt. God has a plan to deliver Israel, and deliver them He will.

And I will give this people favour in the sight of the Egyptians: and it shall come to pass, that, when ye go, ye shall not go empty:

But every woman shall borrow of her neighbour, and of her that sojourneth in her house, jewels of silver, and

jewels of gold, and raiment: and ye shall put them upon your sons, and upon your daughters; and ye shall spoil the Egyptians [Exod. 3:21–22].

The word *borrow* in this passage does not mean to steal but to collect back wages. The Israelites had been slaves without pay. God tells them to collect their back wages for several hundred years' work. They would leave Egypt recompensed for years of toil. God was caring for His people.

CHAPTER 4

THEME: Moses' objections to being Israel's deliverer;
Aaron becomes Moses' spokesman: Moses returns to
Egypt

This chapter tells us of the return of Moses to Egypt and the marvelous way in which God deals with his misgivings. Moses has many questions in his mind and many hurdles to surmount but God has an answer for every objection of Moses.

MOSES' OBJECTIONS TO BEING ISRAEL'S DELIVERER

Moses had several reasons why he felt he was the wrong man for the job God wanted him to do.

And Moses answered and said, But, behold, they will not believe me, nor hearken unto my voice: for they will say, The LORD hath not appeared unto thee.

And the LORD said unto him, What is that in thine hand? And he said, A rod [Exod. 4:1–2].

In the days to come Moses would use the rod in many different ways. It would become his badge of authority. It would be a testimony to Israel and Egypt of God's presence with Moses. It would also serve as a source of strength to him.

And he said, Cast it on the ground. And he cast it on the ground, and it became a serpent; and Moses fled from before it [Exod. 4:3].

When Moses cast the rod to the ground, it became a vicious monster. Note that there is no power in the rod. It is simply an instrument and

can be used by Satan as well as by God. For example, liken a dollar bill
to the rod. The dollar can be used to help pay for a murder or for
prostitution, gambling, liquor, etc. In other words that dollar can become a serpent. Only when that dollar, or the rod, is put in the hand of
a man of God who is moved by the power of God can it be used for
God. This is an important lesson God is teaching in this passage.

> **And the LORD said unto Moses, Put forth thine hand,
> and take it by the tail. And he put forth his hand, and
> caught it, and it became a rod in his hand [Exod. 4:4].**

Many people consider the automobile, radio, and television to be of
the Devil. The Devil can use all of these instruments, but they can also
be used for God. Grab that serpent by the tail, friends! Use your automobile to take some dear saint to church or some of your unsaved
friends to hear the Word of God preached. Support Christian programs on television and radio. Do your part to make the media an
instrument of God rather than an instrument of the devil. You make
them a rod in the hand of God.

God called Moses to deliver the children of Israel from the bondage
of Egypt. He trained him for forty years in the desert and commissioned him at the burning bush. This man, who at one time was so
eager that he ran ahead of God, is now reluctant to accept his God-
given office of deliverer. He began to give God his objections and God
put a rod in his hand. He learns that when the rod is used according to
the will of God in the hand of a man yielded to God, it becomes his
badge of authority. In addition to the rod, however, God gives Moses
another token of assurance and teaches him an important lesson as he
is about to assume the great responsibility of leading Israel out of
Egypt.

> **And the LORD said furthermore unto him, Put now thine
> hand into thy bosom. And he put his hand into his
> bosom: and when he took it out, behold, his hand was
> leprous as snow.**

And he said, Put thine hand into thy bosom again. And he put his hand into his bosom again; and plucked it out of his bosom, and, behold, it was turned again as his other flesh.

And it shall come to pass, if they will not believe thee, neither hearken to the voice of the first sign, that they will believe the voice of the latter sign [Exod. 4:6–8].

The great message here is for Moses in particular. His bosom speaks of his inner life. Proverbs 4:23 says, "Keep thy heart with all diligence; for out of it are the issues of life." In other words, the hand will do the bidding of the heart. God wanted to put the rod in the hand of a man yielded to Him. Now he wants Moses' hand to be in accord with his heart. The Lord made this statement in Matthew 7:17: "Even so every good tree bringeth forth good fruit; but a corrupt tree bringeth forth evil fruit." Then in Luke 6:45 the Lord says, "A good man out of the good treasure of his heart bringeth forth that which is good; and an evil man out of the evil treasure of his heart bringeth forth that which is evil: for of the abundance of the heart his mouth speaketh." God is saying to Moses that He wants his *hand* and his *heart*. God is saying the same thing to us today. God does not want our money and our abilities. God wants you and He wants me. If He gets us, then He will get the rest, too.

Moses put his hand in his bosom and it came out leprous. He put his hand into his bosom again and it came out clean. Out of your heart will ultimately come what you are. God wanted that rod in the hand of a man yielded to Him. He wanted that man's hand to move in the same direction as his yielded heart. This is the great lesson God had for Moses, the children of Israel, and for us today.

And Moses said unto the LORD, O my Lord, I am not eloquent, neither heretofore, nor since thou hast spoken unto thy servant: but I am slow of speech, and of a slow tongue [Exod. 4:10].

Moses now offers another objection. He says, "Lord, you need an eloquent speaker for the job and I cannot speak well." Moses is quite able to speak when it is time, but he is giving an excuse. He feels inadequate.

> And the LORD said unto him, Who hath made man's mouth? or who maketh the dumb, or deaf, or the seeing, or the blind? have not I the LORD?

> Now therefore go, and I will be with thy mouth, and teach thee what thou shalt say [Exod. 4:11–12].

God is telling Moses that He not only wants his hand but He wants his mouth also. He promises to be with Moses' mouth and teach him what to say. Out of the heart proceed the issues of life and "what is in the well of the heart will come up through the bucket of the mouth." God wanted the heart of Moses.

> And he said, O my Lord, send, I pray thee, by the hand of him whom thou wilt send [Exod. 4:13].

Moses is trying to find a substitute.

AARON BECOMES MOSES' SPOKESMAN

> And the anger of the LORD was kindled against Moses, and he said, Is not Aaron the Levite thy brother? I know that he can speak well. And also, behold, he cometh forth to meet thee: and when he seeth thee, he will be glad in his heart.

> And thou shalt speak unto him, and put words in his mouth: and I will be with thy mouth, and with his mouth, and will teach you what ye shall do.

> And he shall be thy spokesman unto the people: and he shall be, even he shall be to thee instead of a mouth, and thou shalt be to him instead of God [Exod. 4:14–16].

Moses made a great mistake in asking God for a spokesman. God allowed it, but He did not want a divided command. You will find out that it caused problems as the children of Israel journeyed through the wilderness. In the Book of Numbers we will discover that Aaron was involved in making a golden calf for Israel to worship while Moses was on Mount Sinai! This was a terrible blunder on the part of Aaron, and it came as the result of a divided command. Other problems crop up in the Book of Numbers. God did not need Aaron for the job of delivering the children of Israel; all He needed was Moses. Moses was reluctant to trust God all the way, and God had to send another man with him. We need to recognize our weakness, but when God calls us to do a job we should respond with trust. God will enable us to do the job He calls us to do.

> **And thou shalt take this rod in thine hand, wherewith thou shalt do signs.**

> **And Moses went and returned to Jethro his father in law, and said unto him, Let me go, I pray thee, and return unto my brethren which are in Egypt, and see whether they be yet alive. And Jethro said to Moses, Go in peace [Exod. 4:17–18].**

MOSES RETURNS TO EGYPT

> **And the LORD said unto Moses in Midian, Go, return into Egypt: for all the men are dead which sought thy life [Exod. 4:19].**

There is a new Pharaoh in Egypt. The Pharaoh who had ordered Moses' death is now dead and Moses can safely return to Egypt.

> **And Moses took his wife and his sons, and set them upon an ass, and he returned to the land of Egypt: and Moses took the rod of God in his hand.**

> And the Lord said unto Moses, When thou goest to re-
> turn into Egypt, see that thou do all those wonders be-
> fore Pharaoh, which I have put in thine hand: but I will
> harden his heart, that he shall not let the people go
> [Exod. 4:20–21].

The fact that God says He will harden Pharaoh's heart has always presented a problem. This problem comes up again when we consider
the plagues, and we will study it then in more detail and arrive at a
satisfactory solution.

> And thou shalt say unto Pharaoh, Thus saith the Lord,
> Israel is my son, even my firstborn [Exod. 4:22].

God did not call the individual Israelite a son of God, but He did say of
the nation, "Israel is my son, even my firstborn."

> And I say unto thee, Let my son go, that he may serve
> me: and if thou refused to let him go, behold, I will slay
> thy son, even thy firstborn [Exod. 4:23].

God was very lenient in dealing with Pharaoh and the Egyptians. He
told Pharaoh at the beginning of the contest, "Either let my son Israel
go or I will slay your son." God sent many plagues before He touched
the firstborn of Egypt, giving him ample time to acknowledge the true
God and let Israel go, but Pharaoh did not avail himself of the opportunity.

> And it came to pass by the way in the inn, that the Lord
> met him, and sought to kill him [Exod. 4:24].

This is a strange verse, but it reveals the third real objection of Moses.
He had neglected to circumcise his sons. Circumcision was the evidence or seal of the covenant of God made with Abraham. If Moses
would proclaim God's will to others, he too had to be obedient to
God's will. God had to forcibly remind Moses of his disobedience.

Then Zipporah took a sharp stone, and cut off the fore-skin of her son, and cast it at his feet, and said, Surely a bloody husband art thou to me.

So he let him go: then she said, A bloody husband thou art, because of the circumcision [Exod. 4:25-26].

This incident is difficult to understand, and we must retrace our steps somewhat to examine the problem. When Moses fled as a fugitive from Egypt, he went to the land of Midian. The Midianites were the offspring of Abraham and Keturah. These people were monotheistic. They were not idolaters but worshiped one God. Moses felt at home with these people. He became close friends with the priest of Midian who had seven daughters. Moses married his daughter Zipporah—a name that sounds like a modern gadget to take the place of buttons. Actually, as we have said before, her name means "sparrow" or "little bird." The wife of Moses was the first "Lady Bird."

God blessed Moses' home in the beginning. His first son Gershom, meaning "stranger", was born in Midian. Moses had been a stranger in his land, but he had made it his home.

In Moses' married life, unfortunately, there was a problem. God called Moses at the burning bush and commissioned him to go to Egypt. Pharaoh was dead and it was safe for Moses to return. As Moses started his journey to Egypt, God attempted to kill him. Why? Moses had neglected the rite of circumcising his son. Circumcision was the badge and seal of God's covenant with Abraham that was designed to teach the Israelites to have no confidence in the flesh. The flesh was to be cut away, and each Israelite was to place his trust in God.

Genesis 15:6, Psalm 106:31, Romans 4:3, and Galatians 3:6 tell us that Abraham believed God and it was counted unto him as righteousness. Isaac and Jacob followed the example of Abraham. They were Israelites by birth, but circumcision was the badge of it. It was an act of faith for them to perform that rite. Circumcision was the evidence that a man was the son of Abraham. It was an evidence of their faith.

Apparently Zipporah had resisted the ordinance of circumcision, and Moses had not insisted upon it. Perhaps Moses did not feel this act was so important, and obviously his wife felt it was a foolish and bloody thing to do. At any rate, Moses did not want to precipitate a marital rift. Moses' wife was not atheistic; she was monotheistic. She was simply resisting the ordinance of God, and Moses did not want to make an issue of it. Moses could stand up against Pharaoh, but he could not stand up against his wife. Moses could tell Israel when they were wrong, but he did not oppose his wife when she was wrong.

Moses obviously thought he could get away with this area of disobedience. He just let it slide like many Christian workers do who neglect their own families while trying to fix up other people's families. God intervened in Moses' life. He waylaid him on the way 'o Egypt and revealed to him the seriousness of the situation. There is a real danger when husband and wife do not agree completely in spiritual matters. That is the reason Scripture warns against believers and non-believers getting married.

It was Zipporah who performed the rite of circumcision upon their son to save the life of Moses. Therefore what she did was an act of faith on her part. She claimed the promise of the covenant with Abraham—the redemption of blood with no confidence in the flesh. After the circumcision of their son, perhaps when they reached Egypt, Moses saw the problem, and sent her back home to be with her father. Later on the wilderness march we shall see that Jethro, Moses' father-in-law, brought Zipporah to him and they were reconciled.

And the Lord said to Aaron, Go into the wilderness to meet Moses. And he went, and met him in the mount of God, and kissed him.

And Moses told Aaron all the words of the Lord who had sent him, and all the signs which he had commanded him.

And Moses and Aaron went and gathered together all the elders of the children of Israel:

And Aaron spake all the words which the LORD had spoken unto Moses, and did the signs in the sight of the people.

And the people believed: and when they heard that the LORD had visited the children of Israel, and that he had looked upon their affliction, then they bowed their heads and worshipped [Exod. 4:27–31].

This is a great worship scene that we have here. These people come now to faith in God. And it will be on this basis that God will lead them out of the land of Egypt.

CHAPTER 5

THEME: Moses' appeal for Israel's deliverance; the increase of Israel's burden; Moses' prayer

Chapter 5 begins the contest with Pharaoh. The plagues are leveled against the idolatry of Egypt. It is actually a battle of God with the gods of Egypt. Moses returned to Egypt after an absence of forty years. The deliverer is prepared now to deliver his people. He was to assemble the elders of Israel, and they were to go to Pharaoh and present their request. Pharaoh refused to let Israel go, and this opened the struggle between God and the gods of Egypt.

The plagues were not haphazard. God did not send a plague of frogs and then say, "I wonder what calamity I should send next." Probably nothing was ever quite so organized and meaningful as these plagues. They were directed very definitely toward the idolatry of Egypt.

Pharaoh asked the question, "Who is the Lord? I do not know Him, and I do not intend to let Israel go." So God introduced Himself and did it by bringing plagues on the land of Egypt. In Exodus 7:5 the Lord makes it very clear what He has in mind: "And the Egyptians shall know that I am the LORD, when I stretch forth mine hand upon Egypt, and bring out the children of Israel from among them." God used the plagues to deliver His people and to let the Egyptians know who He was.

Each plague was leveled at a different god of Egypt. There were thousands of temples, millions of idols, and about three thousand gods in Egypt. That will outdo anything we have in this country today. There was power in the religion of Egypt. The Egyptians were not fools. We have transistor radios, color television, and have been to the moon, but that does not mean we are superior. All of our knowledge is based on that which has been handed down from the past. We have been building upon the knowledge that has come to us through the centuries. Paul makes it clear that there was power in the Egyptian religions in 2 Timothy 3:8 when he says, "Now as Jannes and Jambres withstood Moses, so do these also resist the truth: men of corrupt minds, reprobate concerning the faith." The power in Egyptian religion was satanic and Satan grants power to those who worship him. The oracle at Delphi in the Greek periods is an example of it.

God directed His plagues against the idolatry in Egypt, against Pharaoh, and against Satan. It was a battle of the gods. Exodus 12:12 confirms it: "For I will pass through the land of Egypt this night, and will smite all the firstborn in the land of Egypt, both man and beast; and against all the gods of Egypt I will execute judgment: I am the LORD." God exposed the gods of Egypt as false, and He revealed to Israel His ability to deliver them. These Israelites had been born in the brickyards in the midst of idolatry, and God had to show them that He was superior.

A brief outline of each plague might be helpful at this point in order to see that there was some sense to them. When Moses first stood before Pharaoh, he changed his rod into a serpent. The wise men of Egypt performed the same miracle. This reveals that Satan has definite powers. After this demonstration came the ten plagues.

1. *Water turned to blood* (Exod. 7:19–25): The fertility of the land of Egypt depended upon the overflow of the Nile River to bring it both fertilizer and water. Therefore this river was sacred to the god Osiris—whose all-seeing eye is found in many Egyptian paintings. Pagan rites were held every spring when the river brought life out of death. When the water was turned to blood, it brought death instead of life. The wise men of Egypt also imitated this plague with their sorcery.

2. *The plague of frogs* (Exod. 8:1–15): One of the most beautiful temples in Memphis was the temple to Heka, the ugly frog-headed goddess. It was an offense to kill the sacred frog, but if you found them in your house, bed, food, and underfoot everywhere, as the Egyptians did, you might feel like killing them. But they were sacred. The wise men also duplicated this plague which might indicate that their success up to this point was accomplished by sleight-of-hand tricks or some similar magical device.

3. *The plague of lice* (Exod. 8:16–20): The Egyptians worshiped the earth-god Geb. But "the dust of the land became lice throughout

all the land of Egypt." This which was sacred to Geb they now despise. Pharaoh did not ask that this plague be taken away, and the Egyptian sorcerers could not reproduce this pestilence. They seem to have acknowledged that the One who brought this plague was supreme over the gods of Egypt.

4. *The plague of flies* (Exod. 8:20–32): It is thought by some that the swarms of flies were actually masses of the sacred beetle. And Khepara was the beetle-god. The beetle, or scarab, is found in the Egyptian tombs and speaks of eternal life. These beetles were sacred to Ra the sun-god.

5. *The plague of murrain* (Exod. 9:1–7): Murrain was a disease that affected cattle. The second largest temple that Egypt ever built was located in Memphis and was for the worship of the black bull Apis. You could say that this plague caused the Egyptians to worship a sick cow!

6. *The plague of boils* (Exod. 9:8–17): The priests of all the religions of Egypt had to be spotless—with no mark or blemish on their bodies—in order to serve in the temples. Well, they had a moratorium on worship in Egypt during this period because of the boils that were on all the priests. None of them could serve anywhere. It was actually a judgment on the entire religion of Egypt.

7. *The plague of hail* (Exod. 9:18–35): God demonstrates His power with the plague of hail over the sky-goddess who is powerless in her own domain.

8. *The plague of locusts* (Exod. 10:1–20): The judgment of the locusts was against the insect gods. The plague of locusts meant the crops were cursed. This was an evidence of the judgment of God as found in the books of Joel and Revelation also.

9. *The plague of darkness* (Exod. 10:21–29): God moved in with darkness against the chief god that was worshiped—the sun-god Ra. The sun disc is the most familiar symbol found in Egyptian ruins. The plague of darkness shows the utter helplessness of Ra.

10. *Death of the firstborn* (Exod. 11—12:36): According to the religion of Egypt, the firstborn belonged to the gods of Egypt. In other words, God took what was set aside for the gods of Egypt. God was teaching the Egyptians who He was. He was convincing Pharaoh that

he was God. Also He was bringing His own people to the place where
they were willing to acknowledge Him as their God. This was the
final act of judgment that would free Israel from Egyptian bondage.

It is important to understand that there was purpose in the plagues
of Egypt. God challenged the gods of Egypt to a contest and defeated
them.

You can imagine the idolatry that was in the land of Egypt. Yet God
through Isaiah predicted that the time would come when every idol
would disappear from Egypt. And today Egypt is a Moslem country
that does not permit idols at all. Every idol has disappeared, as God
said they would.

MOSES' APPEAL FOR ISRAEL'S DELIVERANCE

In chapter 5 the contest begins with Pharaoh and the battle begins
with the Egyptian gods.

> And afterward Moses and Aaron went in, and told Phar-
> aoh, Thus saith the LORD God of Israel, Let my people
> go, that they may hold a feast unto me in the wilderness
> [Exod. 5:1].

Sacrificing to God in the wilderness was the first step toward Israel's
freedom. Moses and Aaron did not rush into the presence of Pharaoh
and say, "Let my people go. We are leaving Egypt and going to the
Promised Land." They simply requested that Israel be allowed to go
out into the wilderness and worship. They were preparing Pharaoh
and softening him up for what would ultimately come. Now notice
the reaction of Pharaoh.

> And Pharaoh said, Who is the LORD, that I should obey
> his voice to let Israel go? I know not the LORD, neither
> will I let Israel go [Exod. 5:2].

The expression "Let my people go" has been made famous in a picture. I wish we could make the question "Who is the Lord?" famous. It

is the best question of all today because you have to know Him before there can be any deliverance for you. Pharaoh made two definite statements: (1) I do not know the Lord, and, (2) I do not intend to let Israel go. In a short time Pharaoh would become acquainted with the God of Israel in a terrible way, and he would let the Israelites go.

And they said, The God of the Hebrews hath met with us: let us go, we pray thee, three days' journey into the desert, and sacrifice unto the LORD our God; lest he fall upon us with pestilence, or with the sword [Exod. 5:3].

God wants us to worship Him. He will judge us if we do not take this step now.

And the king of Egypt said unto them, Wherefore do ye, Moses and Aaron, let the people from their works? get you unto your burdens.

And Pharaoh said, Behold, the people of the land now are many, and ye make them rest from their burdens [Exod. 5:4–5].

Moses had been having mass meetings with his people. They were restless and wanted to leave Egypt. Pharaoh saw the problem this presented, and his answer was to send them back to the brickyards. This is exactly what he did and increased their difficulties at the same time.

THE INCREASE OF ISRAEL'S BURDEN

And Pharaoh commanded the same day the taskmasters of the people, and their officers, saying,

Ye shall no more give the people straw to make brick, as heretofore: let them go and gather straw for themselves.

And the tale of the bricks, which they did make heretofore, ye shall lay upon them; ye shall not diminish aught

> thereof: for they be idle; therefore they cry, saying, Let
> us go and sacrifice to our God [Exod. 5:6–8].

Pharaoh thought Israel was asking for a holiday. He reasoned that if
they wanted some time off, they must not be working hard enough.
Straw was withheld from them, and they were forced to produce the
same number of bricks and gather the straw too. Their daily tasks increased so that they served with rigor.

> Then the officers of the children of Israel came and cried
> unto Pharaoh, saying, Wherefore dealest thou thus with
> thy servants?
>
> There is no straw given unto thy servants, and they say
> to us, Make brick: and, behold, thy servants are beaten;
> but the fault is in thine own people.
>
> But he said, Ye are idle, ye are idle: therefore ye say, Let
> us go and do sacrifice to the LORD.
>
> Go therefore now, and work; for there shall no straw be
> given you, yet shall ye deliver the tale of bricks.
>
> And the officers of the children of Israel did see that they
> were in evil case, after it was said, Ye shall not minish
> aught from your bricks of your daily task.
>
> And they met Moses and Aaron, who stood in the way,
> as they came forth from Pharaoh:
>
> And they said unto them, The LORD look upon you, and
> judge; because ye have made our savour to be abhorred
> in the eyes of Pharaoh, and in the eyes of his servants, to
> put a sword in their hand to slay us [Exod. 5:15–21].

The children of Israel blamed Moses and Aaron for their increased
burden. They accused these two men of hindering rather than helping
them and of giving Pharaoh an excuse to make life more unbearable
for them.

MOSES' PRAYER

And Moses returned unto the LORD, and said, Lord,
wherefore has thou so evil entreated this people? why is
it that thou hast sent me?

For since I came to Pharaoh to speak in thy name, he
hath done evil to this people; neither hast thou delivered
thy people at all [Exod. 5:22–23].

Moses is impatient. He is complaining to God. "I've come down
here to deliver them at Your instructions. But instead of letting them
go, Pharaoh has only made life more difficult for the children of Israel." Moses could not see the entire picture, but God was moving
slowly and patiently to work out His plan. In chapter 6 God encour-
ages Moses and the children of Israel and renews His promise to deliver them. God has much to teach Moses, the Israelites, the
Egyptians, and Pharaoh.

CHAPTER 6

THEME: Jehovah's answer to Moses' prayer; a partial genealogy of Israel; renewal of Moses' commission

Chapter 6 is a continuation of the last part of chapter 5. The time for the plagues to descend upon Egypt is at hand. The battle of the gods is about to begin. What has led up to this moment? In retrospect we find that the first thing Moses, Aaron, and the elders of Israel did was ask Pharaoh for permission to go out into the wilderness and sacrifice unto the Lord for three days. Pharaoh's answer was no because he "did not know the Lord." He then increased the burden of the Israelites. The children of Israel complained to Moses who in turn complained to the Lord.

God wanted to assure Moses of who He was and what He was going to do. The God of Abraham, Isaac, and Jacob had heard the groanings of Israel and was going to deliver them. God wanted Moses to look at the past history of Israel and see how He had kept them. God had demonstrated time and time again His love for Israel and His desire to help them. God had intervened many times in their behalf.

God also intervenes in our behalf today. I am certain He has for me—maybe you are not sure of God's working in your life. Philippians 1:6 says: "Being confident of this very thing, that he which hath begun a good work in you will perform it until the day of Jesus Christ." God knows our needs today. He knows our desperate condition. He can and *wants* to help us just as He helped Israel in Egypt.

JEHOVAH'S ANSWER TO MOSES' PRAYER

Jehovah, the self-existing One, speaks to Moses to give him encouragement, hope, and confidence.

> Then the LORD said unto Moses, Now shalt thou see what I will do to Pharaoh: for with a strong hand shall he let

> them go, and with a strong hand shall he drive them out
> of his land [Exod. 6:1].

Jehovah is telling Moses that He is THE LORD. He does not have to
make preparations for the future. He is self-existing and needs no re-
serve. God is not dependent upon anything in creation. He does not
lean upon anything; rather, all of creation leans upon Him for support. God wanted Moses to lean upon Him too.

> **And God spake unto Moses, and said unto him, I am the
> LORD:**
>
> **And I appeared unto Abraham, unto Isaac, and unto
> Jacob, by the name of God Almighty, but by my name
> JEHOVAH was I not known to them.**
>
> **And I have also established my covenant with them, to
> give them the land of Canaan, the land of their pilgrim-
> age, wherein they were strangers.**
>
> **And I have also heard the groaning of the children of
> Israel, whom the Egyptians keep in bondage; and I have
> remembered my covenant [Exod. 6:2–5].**

God is telling Moses that He had appeared to Abraham, Isaac, and
Jacob—but not as Jehovah. God, as Jehovah, was going to redeem His
people, adopt them as His own, deliver them from bondage, and lead
them to the Promised Land. By all of this they would know God as
Jehovah, a part of His character that He had not revealed to Abraham,
Isaac, and Jacob.

In verses 6 to 8 God reveals the seven "I wills" of redemption.
These verses paint a marvelous portrait picture for us today and were
a great encouragement to Moses in that day. God announces who He is
and what He is going to do. We have a Savior today who tells us who
He is and what He is going to do. He is able to save to the uttermost all
who come to Him.

Wherefore say unto the children of Israel, I am the LORD, and I will bring you out from under the burdens of the Egyptians, and I will rid you out of their bondage, and I will redeem you with a stretched out arm, and with great judgments:

And I will take you to me for a people, and I will be to you a God: and ye shall know that I am the LORD your God, which bringeth you out from under the burdens of the Egyptians.

And I will bring you in unto the land, concerning the which I did swear to give it to Abraham, to Isaac, and to Jacob; and I will give it you for an heritage: I am the LORD [Exod. 6:6-8].

The seven "I wills" of redemption are:
1. I will bring you out from under the burdens of the Egyptians.
2. I will rid you out of their bondage.
3. I will redeem you with an outstretched arm.
4. I will take you to me for a people.
5. I will be to you a God.
6. I will bring you into the land.
7. I will give it to you for an heritage.

I will bring you out from under your burdens: The corollary and parallel to our redemption in Christ is found in this statement. We carry a burden of sin today. The things of the world are an oppression to the heart. We are told not to love the world. God can deliver us from the burden of sin through faith in Jesus Christ.

I will rid you out of bondage: God will deliver you from the *slavery* of sin. I received a remarkable letter from a man that bears out the fact that God is able to deliver from the bondage of sin. This man is brilliant but he lived in sin. He has had at least six illegitimate children as the result of affairs with that many women. And the work by which he made a living was not altogether honest. This fellow had as checkered a career as anyone I have ever heard about. Then he began listening to our *Thru The Bible* radio broadcast day after day, and the Word of God reached into his life. As he drank in the truths of the Bible, the darkness began to roll away, and the light broke through into his heart and life. He realized he was not trusting the Lord Jesus Christ as his Savior. God redeemed this man. Redemption is His business.

The Israelites were in the land of Egypt living a life of bondage. God said, "I am going to take you out of this place. I am going to rid you of your bondage."

I will redeem you with an outstretched arm: This is the mighty bared arm spoken of by Isaiah the prophet: "Who hath believed our report? and to whom is the arm of the LORD revealed?" (Isa. 53:1) Well, I don't know to whom it is being revealed. God is doing a work of redemption in the hearts and lives of men and women today. Each of us needs a Savior from sin because we are corrupt in His sight. He loved us enough to die for us in order that we might be saved. If He was willing to do that, we must be willing to come as sinners to the Lord. If we place our faith in the work of Jesus Christ for us, we will be saved. God has a great plan of salvation but man must come to Him for it. He will redeem you with an outstretched arm.

I will take you to me for a people: Just think—God has lifted us out of the muck and mire of sin and made us His sons by faith in Christ Jesus! Now He tells us, "I will be to you a God." God does not save us and then run off and leave us. He wants to be our God. If you are really saved, you will not go on living as if God does not exist. If you have trusted Jesus Christ as Savior, it will transform your life. He will become your God and you will bow down to Him and acknowledge who He is. God wants to redeem you. He wants you to know Christ as Savior and Lord. He wants you to know you are saved. He wants to be your God. He wants us for His people.

I will be to you a God: God chose believers in Christ before the foundation of the world which places it before all time—in eternity past. The reason for the choice was not found in the believers, but in the all-wise purpose of God. He does not struggle to love His own in spite of their failures. God loves His own because it is His nature to love. He wants to be our God.

I will bring you into the land: The land is Canaan. It was promised by God to Abraham, Isaac, and Jacob. Canaan is not a picture of heaven. It is a picture of the Christian life as believers should be living it. Canaan typifies the heavenlies where we are blessed with all spiritual blessing—the believer has to walk worthy of his high calling for perfect enjoyment of spiritual blessing. This is done through the filling of the Spirit (Eph. 4:1—5:18). There are also warfare and battles to win. Believers sometimes live as if they are bankrupt in the wilderness of the world and never enter into the riches of His grace and mercy. Are you living today in the life, light, and love of a living Savior?

I will give you the land for an heritage: Paul, in the fifth chapter of Romans, makes it clear that we have been justified by faith and have peace with God through the Lord Jesus Christ. We have access to Him. We have joy in the midst of trouble. We have been given the Holy Spirit of God to indwell us, and the love of God has been made real to us. We have been delivered from the wrath to come and are saved from the Great Tribulation period. What kind of salvation do you have, friend, that you talk about but has not transformed your life or redeemed you from something? These verses tell of our heritage and picture our salvation.

And Moses spake so unto the children of Israel: but they hearkened not unto Moses for anguish of spirit, and for cruel bondage [Exod. 6:9].

Your heart must go out to the children of Israel at a time like this. They found it impossible to believe Moses because he had not helped their cause but had only been responsible for their increased burden.

And the LORD spake unto Moses, saying,

Go in, speak unto Pharaoh king of Egypt, that he let the children of Israel go out of his land.

And Moses spake before the LORD, saying, Behold, the children of Israel have not hearkened unto me; how then shall Pharaoh hear me, who am of uncircumcised lips?

And the LORD spake unto Moses and unto Aaron, and
gave them a charge unto the children of Israel, and unto
Pharaoh king of Egypt, to bring the children of Israel
out of the land of Egypt [Exod. 6:10–13].

Moses was not accepted by the children of Israel; he was not accepted
by Pharaoh. God told him to speak to Pharaoh again and Moses is
reluctant to go. His eyes are on the circumstances rather than on God.

A PARTIAL GENEALOGY OF ISRAEL

In the midst of all these difficulties and circumstances we come to a
very strange occurrence. God is careful to list the families of Israel
again—an important item as far as the Old Testament is concerned.
Frankly, reading all these names is boring to me and puts me to sleep,
but they are important and thrilling to God. He is insistent that the
genealogies be recorded. God wants us to know who we are reading
about and who His children are. God feels the same way about you
and me. He wants us to be the sons of God through faith in Christ.

These be the heads of their fathers' houses: The sons of
Reuben the firstborn of Israel. . . . And the sons of Simeon. . . . And these are the names of the sons of Levi
according to their generations; Gershon, and Kohath,
and Merari; and the years of the life of Levi were an
hundred thirty and seven years [Exod. 6:14–16].

Gershon, Kohath, and Merari are the three sons of Levi. They are the
men who will take the tabernacle through the wilderness.

And the sons of Kohath; Amram, and Izhar, and He-
bron, and Uzziel. . . . [Exod. 6:18].

Moses had not mentioned his parents by name. They were ordinary
people, and they were in slavery. They were members of the tribe of
Levi. That is all Moses told us.

> **And Amram took him Jochebed his father's sister to wife; and she bare him Aaron and Moses: and the years of the life of Amram were an hundred and thirty and seven years [Exod. 6:20].**

In this passage the parents of Aaron and Moses are named—Amram and his wife Jochebed. The question has been asked, "Why wasn't the life of Aaron in as much jeopardy as the life of Moses when the command to kill the Hebrew babies was given by Pharaoh?" The answer is simply that Aaron was older than Moses, and the decree had not been made yet. It was not until Pharaoh saw how quickly the Israelites were increasing in number that he issued his orders.

The next few verses continue to deal with the genealogy and I want to pick up my train of thought with verse 26.

> **These are that Aaron and Moses, to whom the LORD said, Bring out the children of Israel from the land of Egypt according to their armies.**

> **These are they which spake to Pharaoh king of Egypt, to bring out the children of Israel from Egypt: these are that Moses and Aaron [Exod. 6:26–27].**

We saw in verse 12 that Moses was discouraged. Neither the circumcised nor the uncircumcised will accept him. At this juncture God steps in and gives the background of who Moses is. He has to live up to his claims before he can deliver the children of Israel.

There are those today who say that it is not essential to believe the virgin birth of Christ. I say that it is absolutely essential to believe it. It is part of the credentials of Christ. You do not have to trust in His virgin birth to be saved—when I came to Christ I had never *heard* of the virgin birth. You must trust in His death and resurrection to be saved. But when you are saved, you will come to know Him. And when you know Him, you'll find out He's virgin born. If He was not virgin born, then you have made a mistake in trusting Him because He is not who He claims to be. No one who is truly saved will deny the virgin birth of Jesus Christ.

It is also essential that Moses and Aaron are who they claim to be.
It has been forty years since Moses left Egypt. In the meantime he has
married the daughter of the priest of Midian. Now here he is back in
Egypt. Who is he anyway? This genealogy tells who he is. He belongs
to the tribe of Levi, and his father and mother are Amram and Jochebed. The genealogy provides the necessary credentials for Moses to
accomplish the work he is sent to do in the land of Egypt.

RENEWAL OF MOSES' COMMISSION

On the basis of the credentials, God renews His call to Moses and
Aaron.

> **And it came to pass on the day when the LORD spake
> unto Moses in the land of Egypt,**

> **That the LORD spakᵔ unto Moses, saying, I am the LORD:
> speak thou unto Pharaoh king of Egypt all that I say
> unto thee.**

> **And Moses said before the LORD, Behold, I am of uncir-
> cumcised lips, and how shall Pharaoh hearken unto
> me? [Exod. 6:28–30].**

Moses is making excuses again. It is not a very pleasant task he has to
perform. He has been rejected all along the way. Even after he shows
his credentials of being in the tribe of Levi, he is rejected. Now Levi
was the son of Jacob, Jacob was the son of Isaac, and Isaac was the son
of Abraham. God made the promises concerning the children of Israel
to Abraham. "I'm in the right line," says Moses, "but I hesitate to go."
Moses does not have much faith.

CHAPTER 7

THEME: The renewal of Moses' commission—continued; the Egyptian magicians; the first plague—water turned to blood

The battle between the Lord God of Israel and the Egyptian gods has not yet been joined, but we are coming to it now. God has been preparing the children of Israel, Moses and Aaron, and even old Pharaoh for the engagement.

Moses is going to stand before Pharaoh, but Aaron will do the speaking. Was Moses tongue-tied, did he stutter, or did he have some other speech impediment? My personal feeling is that Moses' problem was psychological. After forty years in the wilderness he may have felt inadequate and fearful.

God wanted to make it very clear, however, that He, and not Moses, was going to deliver the children of Israel. By the way, that is one reason it is so difficult for God to move today in our individual lives in the church. There is always some person or some organization who is taking the credit. When we are always getting in the way to take the credit, the mighty bared arm of God is not revealed. God had to put the human element out of the way because He cannot use the flesh. God, speaking through the apostle Paul, tells us this in Romans 7:18, "For I know that in me (that is, in my flesh,) dwelleth no good thing: for to will is present with me; but how to perform that which is good I find not." It is difficult for some people to believe that there is no good in man because they rather count on it, especially in a time of emergency. But God does not want our flesh. He cannot use it; He will not use it. God has set the flesh aside, and Aaron will speak for Moses.

THE RENEWAL OF MOSES' COMMISSION—CONTINUED

And the Lord said unto Moses, See I have made thee a god to Pharaoh: and Aaron thy brother shall be thy prophet [Exod. 7:1].

This is one of the finest definitions you will find of a prophet. Moses was going to be a god to Pharaoh. Aaron was going to be the spokesman for Moses. Aaron would be a prophet. A prophet is one who speaks for God, one who has a message from God to the people. A prophet is the opposite of a priest. He comes out from God and goes to the people, but a priest represents the people before God. A priest is not to speak for God and a prophet is not to represent the people. He is to represent God. Aaron is to represent Moses before the people, and Moses is to represent God before both the people and Pharaoh.

> **Thou shalt speak all that I command thee: and Aaron thy brother shall speak unto Pharaoh, that he send the children of Israel out of his land.**
>
> **And I will harden Pharaoh's heart, and multiply my signs and my wonders in the land of Egypt [Exod. 7:2–3].**

What does it mean to harden Pharaoh's heart? Did God harden Pharaoh's heart? Yes, but in this way: If Pharaoh were a tenderhearted, sweet fellow who desired to turn to God and was happy to have Moses deliver the children of Israel because Pharaoh wanted to do something for them, then it was mean of God to harden the heart of this wonderful Pharaoh. If that is the way you read it, friends, you are not reading it right. The hardening is a figurative word, which can mean twisting, as with a rope. It means God twisted the heart of Pharaoh. He was going to squeeze out what was in it. God forced him to do the thing he really wanted to do.

Pharaoh was like the politicians of today who will not say what they actually mean. They feel one way and speak another way. Pharaoh did not want to let the children of Israel go, and yet he wanted to appear as a benevolent ruler. He wanted everyone to think he was a generous man, but in this matter of Israel he was hard. Well, God is going to bring Pharaoh into court and make him admit how he really feels.

There are certain men who have to be taken into court before they will do what they have already agreed to do. A Los Angeles contractor told me that he had to take a man to court before the man would honor a contract. He would not fulfill his obligations until the law got after him. That is what God is doing to Pharaoh. God is bringing Pharaoh into court and saying, "You are going to reveal the thing that is actually in your heart. You cannot say one thing and do something else." God is going to force the king's hand in this particular matter. By the way, this is exactly what God is going to do with every individual that will someday come into His presence. You will be seen as you really are. There will be no more camouflage. This is a rather frightening thing for some of us, is it not?

> But Pharaoh shall not hearken unto you, that I may lay my hand upon Egypt, and bring forth mine armies, and my people the children of Israel, out of the land of Egypt by great judgments.
>
> And the Egyptians shall know that I am the Lord, when I stretch forth mine hand upon Egypt, and bring out the children of Israel from among them [Exod. 7:4–5].

In other words, Pharaoh will stand revealed for what he is, and the Lord God of Israel will be revealed for who He is. The Egyptians will know, and the Israelites will have it confirmed, and Moses and Aaron will be justified.

> And Moses and Aaron did as the Lord commanded them, so did they.
>
> And Moses was fourscore years old, and Aaron fourscore and three years old, when they spake unto Pharaoh [Exod. 7:6–7].

Aaron was three years older than Moses.

> And the Lord spake unto Moses and unto Aaron, saying

> When Pharaoh shall speak unto you, saying, Shew a
> miracle for you: then thou shalt say unto Aaron, Take
> thy rod, and cast it before Pharaoh, and it shall become
> a serpent [Exod. 7:8–9].

Pharaoh is probably going to ask Moses and Aaron, "Where are your credentials? You have come before me and made this excessive demand upon me; now show me your authority." Aaron's rod was to be the badge of authority.

THE EGYPTIAN MAGICIANS

> And Moses and Aaron went in unto Pharaoh, and they
> did so as the LORD had commanded: and Aaron cast
> down his rod before Pharaoh, and before his servants,
> and it became a serpent [Exod. 7:10].

There is some question about the word *serpent* in this passage because there is very little history concerning the snake in Egypt. Actually the word used here is *crocodile*. During the days of Moses there were many of these creatures living in the Nile River and ponds throughout the land. The rod changed into a crocodile.

You will find as we study the plagues that God was dealing with the whole realm of zoology. That is, the gods of Egypt were either animal or bird or insect. Paul wrote about it when he said, "Professing themselves to be wise, they became fools, and changed the glory of the uncorruptible God into an image made like to corruptible man, and to birds, and fourfooted beasts, and creeping things" (Rom. 1:22–23).

The Egyptians symbolized everything. They took an abstract idea and put it into the concrete form of an image. They had deities which represented every phase and function of life. They did not miss a thing. They changed monotheism into polytheism. As Sir Wallis Budge has stated it, "They believed in the existence of one great God, self-produced, self-existent, almighty, and eternal." Unfortunately, they felt "that this Being was too great and mighty to concern Himself with the affairs and destinies of human beings." Therefore He "permitted the management of this world . . . to fall into the hands of hordes of 'gods' and demons, and good and bad spirits." This is what the Egyptians believed.

This is the very thing Paul found when he went to Athens. He found a monument to the "unknown God." "For as I passed by, and beheld your devotions, I found an altar with this inscription, TO THE UNKNOWN GOD. Whom therefore ye ignorantly worship, him declare I unto you" (Acts 17:23). If a man worships all of these different gods, he cannot know the living and true God. So the Lord God of Israel attacks the gods of Egypt to show who He is.

The Hebrew word *tannin* translated "serpent" in this chapter is not translated "serpent" anywhere else in the Bible. In the books of Isaiah and Ezekiel it is rendered "dragon." The word is actually satanic in its meaning, and that is probably why the translators used the word *serpent*. Regardless of the reason, the fact remains that the Egyptians worshiped the crocodile. It occupied a large place in the worship and religion of Egypt. Sebak was a deity of evil with a crocodile head. Apepi, the perpetual arch enemy of all the solar gods, appeared in the form of a crocodile. The Egyptians engaged in a magical ritual which was performed in the temple of Amen-Ra in the city of Thebes. Apepi lived in the nethermost part of the heaven and endeavored every day to prevent the rising of the sun-god Ra. He stirred up lightning, thunder, tempests, storms, hurricanes, rain, and tried to obscure the light of the sun by filling the sky with clouds, mists, fog and blackness. The Egyptian ritual was an attempt to destroy Apepi. It was a prominent worship of Egypt and the first thing against which God delivers a blow. Aaron's rod is changed into a crocodile!

Then Pharaoh also called the wise men and the sorcerers: now the magicians of Egypt, they also did in like manner with their enchantments [Exod. 7:11].

The magicians of Egypt duplicated the miracle of Aaron's rod. Perhaps it would be better to say they imitated the miracle. Whatever and however they did it, they made a pretty good show of it. Paul, however, has a word to say about it in 2 Timothy 3:8, "Now as Jannes and Jambres withstood Moses, so do these also resist the truth: men of corrupt minds, reprobate concerning the faith." These magicians resisted the living and true God.

> For they cast down every man his rod, and they became serpents: but Aaron's rod swallowed up their rods.
>
> And he hardened Pharaoh's heart, that he hearkened not unto them: as the LORD had said [Exod. 7:12–13].

It is interesting that the Egyptians worship the crocodile and it is Aaron's rod that swallows up their crocodiles. This should have impressed Pharaoh, but it did not. Pharaoh hardened his heart and persisted in his set ways.

THE FIRST PLAGUE—WATER TURNED TO BLOOD

> And the LORD said unto Moses, Pharaoh's heart is hardened, he refuseth to let the people go.
>
> Get thee unto Pharaoh in the morning; lo, he goeth out unto the water; and thou shalt stand by the river's brink against he come; and the rod which was turned to a serpent shalt thou take in thine hand.
>
> And thou shalt say unto him, The LORD God of the Hebrews hath sent me unto thee, saying, Let my people go, that they may serve me in the wilderness: and, behold, hitherto thou wouldest not hear.
>
> Thus saith the LORD, In this thou shalt know that I am the LORD: behold, I will smite with the rod that is in mine hand upon the waters which are in the river, and they shall be turned to blood.
>
> And the fish that is in the river shall die, and the river shall stink; and the Egyptians shall loathe to drink of the water of the river.

And the LORD spake unto Moses, Say unto Aaron, Take
thy rod, and stretch out thine hand upon the waters of
Egypt, upon their streams, upon their rivers, and upon
their ponds, and upon all their pools of water, that they
may become blood; and that there may be blood
throughout all the land of Egypt, both in vessels of
wood, and in vessels of stone [Exod. 7:14–19].

This is another blow at worship in Egypt. The sacred Nile River is
turned to blood. The Egyptians depicted the Nile as Hapi, a fat man
with the breasts of a woman which indicated the powers of fertility
and nourishment. There was a hymn they sang in the temple to this
god which went something like this:

> Thou waterest the fields with Ra created . . .
> Thou art the bringer of food . . . creator
>   of all good things.
> Thou fillest the storehouses . . .
> Thou hast care for the poor and needy.

The Nile River was the life-blood of Egypt. But it had to be water to
be their "life-blood." Now that river is blood and becomes death to
them. What had been a blessing in Egypt is now a curse. This is God's
judgment.

And the magicians of Egypt did so with their enchantments: and Pharaoh's heart was hardened, neither did
he hearken unto them; as the LORD had said.

And Pharaoh turned and went into his house, neither
did he set his heart to this also.

And all the Egyptians digged round about the river for
water to drink; for they could not drink of the water of
the river.

And seven days were fulfilled, after that the LORD had
smitten the river [Exod. 7:22–25].

This plague lasted for seven days. Pharaoh was not convinced this
was the hand of God because his magicians were able to duplicate the
plague. This is an amazing thing! It was a manifestation of the power
of Satan, of course, but they were powerless to change the blood back
into pure water.

CHAPTER 8

THEME: The second plague—frogs; the third plague—lice; the fourth plague—flies

The plagues continue upon the land of Egypt. God is directing His attack against a people immersed in idolatry.

THE SECOND PLAGUE—FROGS

Frogs were represented by Heka, a frog-headed goddess. Also Hapi was depicted as holding a frog out of whose mouth flowed a stream of nourishment. This indicates the close relationship between the god of the Nile and the frog goddess, one of the oldest and the mother of goddesses. She was the goddess of fertility and rebirth, the patroness of midwives. One Egyptian picture shows Heka reciting spells to effect the resurrection of Osiris. Also a carving shows her kneeling before the queen and superintending at the birth of Hatshepset.

> And the LORD spake unto Moses, Go unto Pharaoh, and say unto him, Thus saith the LORD, Let my people go, that they may serve me.
>
> And if thou refuse to let them go, behold, I will smite all thy borders with frogs:
>
> And the river shall bring forth frogs abundantly, which shall go up and come into thine house, and into thy bedchamber, and upon thy bed, and into the house of thy servants, and upon thy people, and into thine ovens, and into thy kneadingtroughs:
>
> And the frogs shall come up both on thee, and upon thy people, and upon all thy servants.

> And the LORD spake unto Moses, Say unto Aaron,
> Stretch forth thine hand with thy rod over the streams,
> over the rivers, and over the ponds, and cause frogs to
> come up upon the land of Egypt [Exod. 8:1-5].

Frogs were everywhere—in Egyptian bedrooms, in kitchens, in every
room in the house, in kneading troughs and in ovens. When they
walked, they walked on frogs; when they sat, they sat on frogs. It was a
terrible situation. One frog could not do very much, but many frogs
caused great consternation. Of course they were sacred and should
not be killed.

> And Aaron stretched out his hand over the waters of
> Egypt; and the frogs came up, and covered the land of
> Egypt.
>
> And the magicians did so with their enchantments, and
> brought up frogs upon the land of Egypt [Exod. 8:6-7].

Once again the Egyptian magicians duplicated the plague of frogs.
This reveals the power of Satan.

> Then Pharaoh called for Moses and Aaron, and said,
> Entreat the LORD, that he may take away the frogs from
> me, and from my people; and I will let the people go,
> that they may do sacrifice unto the LORD.
>
> And Moses said unto Pharaoh, Glory over me: when
> shall I entreat for thee, and for thy servants, and for thy
> people, to destroy the frogs from thee and thy houses,
> that they may remain in the river only?
>
> And he said, To-morrow. And he said, Be it according to
> thy word: that thou mayest know that there is none like
> unto the LORD our God.
>
> And the frogs shall depart from thee, and from thy
> houses, and from thy servants, and from thy people;
> they shall remain in the river only [Exod. 8:8-11].

It is interesting to note that although the magicians could multiply the frogs, they could not remove them. Pharaoh was so upset by this plague that he was ready to promise anything. God was beginning to force this king to acknowledge who He is.

> And Moses and Aaron went out from Pharaoh: and Moses cried unto the LORD because of the frogs which he had brought against Pharaoh.
>
> And the LORD did according to the word of Moses; and the frogs died out of the houses, out of the villages, and out of the fields.
>
> And they gathered them together upon heaps: and the land stank.
>
> But when Pharaoh saw that there was respite, he hardened his heart, and hearkened not unto them; as the LORD had said [Exod. 8:12–15].

This passage gives us a more comprehensive picture of the hardening of Pharaoh's heart. We are told that he hardened his own heart. God's part in this was to bring to the surface that which was already there.

THE THIRD PLAGUE—LICE

> And the LORD said unto Moses, Say unto Aaron, Stretch out thy rod, and smite the dust of the land, that it may become lice throughout all the land of Egypt.
>
> And they did so; for Aaron stretched out his hand with his rod, and smote the dust of the earth, and it became lice in man, and in beast; all the dust of the land became lice throughout all the land of Egypt.
>
> And the magicians did so with their enchantments to bring forth lice, but they could not: so there were lice upon man, and upon beast.

> Then the magicians said unto Pharaoh, This is the fin-
> ger of God: and Pharaoh's heart was hardened, and he
> hearkened not unto them; as the LORD had said [Exod.
> 8:16–19].

Up to this point the magicians were able to duplicate every miracle wrought by the hand of God. For some reason they were powerless to reproduce this plague. If it was by trickery that they duplicated the miracles, at least during this plague they finally acknowledged the finger of God in the plagues. Gradually God was convincing the Egyptians that He alone was God.

The worship of these gods entered into the very life of the Egyptians and into their daily routines. This judgment brought loathing upon Geb, the earth god. Geb was closely related to the earth in all of its states. Geb was the one who made his report to Osiris on the state of the harvest.

The word *lice* could mean gnats or mosquitoes. Its root means to "cover" or "nip" or "pinch." It is interesting that the nipping, pinching, or covering could not be fulfilled by a gnat or a mosquito. It is, however, a good description of lice. A leading zoologist has said that the mites form an enormous order whose leading function, to a large extent, is to play the scavenger. You can well imagine with the land stinking with frogs that there were crowds of lice. The lice could eventually rid the land of the frogs and could therefore become a blessing as well as a curse.

Regardless of the apparent help the lice might have been, one man tells about his experience with them in Egypt: "I noticed that the sand appeared to be in motion. Close . . . inspection revealed . . . that the surface of the ground was a moving mass of minute ticks, thousands of which were crawling up my legs . . . I beat a hasty retreat, pondering the words of the Scriptures, 'the dust of the land became lice throughout all the land of Egypt.'"

The plague of lice could not be duplicated by the Egyptian magicians. God is beginning to level His judgment against life itself in the land of Egypt.

THE FOURTH PLAGUE—FLIES

And the LORD said unto Moses, Rise up early in the morning, and stand before Pharaoh; lo, he cometh forth to the water; and say unto him, Thus saith the LORD, Let my people go, that they may serve me.

Else, if thou wilt not let my people go, behold, I will send swarms of flies upon thee, and upon thy servants, and upon thy people, and into thy houses: and the houses of the Egyptians shall be full of swarms of flies, and also the ground whereon they are.

And I will sever in that day the land of Goshen, in which my people dwell, that no swarms of flies shall be there; to the end thou mayest know that I am the LORD in the midst of the earth.

And I will put a division between my people and thy people: to-morrow shall this sign be [Exod. 8:20–23].

Up until this time the plagues had touched both the lands of Egypt and Goshen where the children of Israel lived. Many people were probably telling Pharaoh that since Goshen was also affected by the plagues, the phenomena of the plagues had a natural explanation. Maybe they attributed the vexation to one of the Egyptian gods. Everything becomes crystal clear at this juncture, however, when God declares that from now on there is to be a distinction, and none of the following plagues will touch the land of Goshen, the home of Israel. From now on, judgment will fall only upon the land of Egypt.

The fourth judgment is the plague of flies. These "flies" were most likely the sacred beetle or scarab as they were known in Egypt. These scarabs, many of gold, are found in the tombs in Egypt. They were sacred to the sun-god Ra. The severity of this plague is reflected in the fact that Pharaoh was willing to reach some sort of compromise with Moses at this time. Notice the proposal that Pharaoh made as the sacred beetle invaded the land.

> And the LORD did so; and there came a grievous swarm
> of flies into the house of Pharaoh, and into his servants'
> houses, and into all the land of Egypt: the land was cor-
> rupted by reason of the swarm of flies.
>
> And Pharaoh called for Moses and for Aaron, and said,
> Go ye, sacrifice to your God in the land.
>
> And Moses said, It is not meet so to do; for we shall sac-
> rifice the abomination of the Egyptians to the LORD our
> God: lo, shall we sacrifice the abomination of the Egyp-
> tians before their eyes, and will they not stone us?
>
> We will go three days' journey into the wilderness, and
> sacrifice to the LORD our God, as he shall command us
> [Exod. 8:24–27].

The Egyptian scarab spoke of eternal life. Imagine this most sacred
thing becoming a curse to the people and a plague upon the land.
Pharaoh wanted to work out a compromise; he made four compromises in all before the plagues came to an end. Moses and Aaron
wanted the children of Israel to go three days' journey into the wilderness and sacrifice. Pharaoh said, "All right, you may sacrifice, but
stay in the land." This is the same kind of compromise that many
Christians make. It is always satanic. This compromise says we can be
Christians but not narrow ones. Be a broad-minded Christian and
don't change your life. If your life doesn't change, you are not a Christian. Now don't accuse me of saying you have to perform good works
to be a Christian. I didn't say it that way. We are saved by faith in
Christ and nothing else—works are excluded. But when you put your
faith in Christ to save you, it will change your life. That is where
Christian conduct comes in. The inner man must be changed first. My
point is that the contemporary church has made many compromises
and for the most part is still in the land of Egypt. You cannot tell the
difference today between the average Christian and the average man of
the world.

The facts tell us that over fifty percent of the citizens of the United States are members of some religious body. Whenever I am on a plane and they are serving cocktails, I play a game to pass the time. At first I counted the people having cocktails but that became too big an undertaking; so now I just count the people who do not have drinks. The other day I was on a plane where only four people did not take cocktails. Now friends, there must have been some church members on that airplane. They were sacrificing in the land of Egypt. They were broad-minded and did not want to be "square." They wanted to live like the world.

We are in a race today with two horses. One horse is black and one is white. If you decide to ride them and put one foot on one horse and one foot on the other, you will soon make a strange discovery. These horses will run in opposite directions. You must make up your mind which horse you want to ride. Moses will not accept Pharaoh's compromise. Moses insists on Israel's going three days' journey into the wilderness to sacrifice to the Lord God.

Next Pharaoh decides on a second compromise.

> **And Pharaoh said, I will let you go, that ye may sacrifice to the Lord your God in the wilderness; only ye shall not go very far away: entreat for me [Exod. 8:28].**

Pharaoh's concession this time is just a shade different from his other one. He says, "Do not go very far away and also entreat for me." This, again, is the same kind of compromise that we find many churches (even fundamental ones) adopting—the program of the world. They run their entire program on the basis of banquets, promotion, contests, and so forth. Many churches are so much like the world that it is difficult to tell them from the Rotary Club, or any knife-and-fork club whose membership is made up largely of those who do not know Christ.

> **And Moses said, Behold, I go out from thee, and I will entreat the Lord that the swarms of flies may depart**

from Pharaoh, from his servants, and from his people, to-morrow: but let not Pharaoh deal deceitfully any more in not letting the people go to sacrifice to the LORD.

And Moses went out from Pharaoh, and entreated the LORD.

And the LORD did according to the word of Moses; and he removed the swarms of flies from Pharaoh, from his servants, and from his people; there remained not one.

And Pharaoh hardened his heart at this time also, neither would he let the people go [Exod. 8:29–32].

Pharaoh is hardening his heart and God is making him reveal what is already in his heart.

CHAPTER 9

THEME: The fifth plague—murrain; the sixth plague—boils; the seventh plague—hail

God continues to deal with the stubborn heart of Pharaoh and with his people. So long as Pharaoh resists the Lord God, anguish and disaster will be poured out upon the land of Egypt and its inhabitants. Up to this chapter we are told that Pharaoh hardened his own heart, and now we are told that God hardened Pharaoh's heart. Pharaoh's continual refusal to acknowledge the Lord God and obey His wishes has brought about God's power in destruction. God wants to shower blessings upon us and wants to save us, but our refusal can turn blessing to cursing. So is the case with Pharaoh.

THE FIFTH PLAGUE—MURRAIN

Then the LORD said unto Moses, Go in unto Pharaoh, and tell him, Thus saith the LORD God of the Hebrews, Let my people go, that they may serve me.

For if thou refuse to let them go, and wilt hold them still,

Behold, the hand of the LORD is upon thy cattle which is in the field, upon the horses, upon the asses, upon the camels, upon the oxen, and upon the sheep: there shall be a very grievous murrain.

And the LORD shall sever between the cattle of Israel and the cattle of Egypt: and there shall nothing die of all that is the children's of Israel.

And the LORD appointed a set time, saying, To-morrow the LORD shall do this thing in the land.

And the LORD did that thing on the morrow, and all the cattle of Egypt died: but of the cattle of the children of Israel died not one.

And Pharaoh sent, and, behold, there was not one of the cattle of the Israelites dead. And the heart of Pharaoh was hardened, and he did not let the people go [Exod. 9:1–7].

A person would think that by this time Pharaoh would be impressed and let the children of Israel go. The fact is obvious that God is involved in this plague and that He is dealing with this king and his people.

With a tour group I made a trip out to the pyramids. When we got back, one of the men who knew the area said, "Did you see the mummies of the bulls?" We said, "No." "Well," he said, "you missed the most important thing." So several in our group went back out there to get pictures of them. I was not interested in going twelve miles in all that heat to see mummies of bulls! But they are there—literally hundreds of them, reverently entombed in sarcophagi. Archaeologists have just begun unearthing them. Apis, the black bull, was worshiped in Egypt. The second largest temple that Egypt built was located in Memphis and was for the worship of the black bull Apis. Apis was supposed to be an embodiment of Ptah of Memphis. Apis, thought to be engendered by a moonbeam, was distinguished by several characteristics. A new Apis was always believed to be born upon the death of the old. The dead bull was embalmed and buried in Memphis. His soul then passed to the world beyond as Osiris-Apis.

You might say that what they had here is the worship of a sick cow. God must have smiled at this. God is leveling His judgments against this awful, frightful institution of idolatry that had such a hold upon the Egyptian people as well as on the Israelites. We shall see later that Israel, too, had gone into idolatry.

THE SIXTH PLAGUE—BOILS

And the LORD said unto Moses and unto Aaron, Take to
you handfuls of ashes of the furnace, and let Moses
sprinkle it toward the heaven in the sight of Pharaoh.

And it shall become small dust in all the land of Egypt,
and shall be a boil breaking forth with blains upon
man, and upon beast, throughout all the land of Egypt.

And they took ashes of the furnace, and stood before
Pharaoh; and Moses sprinkled it up toward heaven; and
it became a boil breaking forth with blains upon man,
and upon beast [Exod. 9:8-10].

It is only an assumption, but this plague probably began right in the
presence of Pharaoh, and he may have been the first one to get boils.

And the magicians could not stand before Moses because of the boils; for the boil was upon the magicians,
and upon all the Egyptians [Exod. 9:11].

Pharaoh had with him at all times his magicians or wise men who
counselled him. They were able to duplicate the first three plagues
and miracles. The rest they were unable to duplicate, and now in this
judgment they have boils too! I can imagine they left in a hurry.

For the first time God is touching man as well as beast with judgment. He is afflicting man's physical body. The priests who served in
the Egyptian temples had to be clean, without any type of breaking
out or sickness. Suddenly this plague of boils comes upon them and
they are unclean, unfit to serve in the temples. This brings to a halt all
of the false worship in Egypt.

I walked over part of the ruins of the city of Memphis. The ruins
are practically all gone now, but archaeologists know something of the
extent of that great city. Up one thoroughfare and down the other was
temple after temple. There were over one thousand temples in Mem-

phis, and priests served in all of them. You can imagine what this
plague of boils did to the services in these temples. Everything
slowed to a standstill. All the bright lights went off!

About the time I was in this city I remember reading about a strike
in Las Vegas. There on "glitter gulch" are probably more neon lights
than any place in the world. I have been told that if you fly in an airplane over Las Vegas at night, it is so bright that you think the sun is
coming up. Well, they had a strike and the lights went out. Motels
closed and the people left. It was such a startling event that the strike
was settled immediately.

Conditions were similar in the land of Egypt to those in Las Vegas
during the strike. False religion was out of business. Everyone had
boils. The priests could not serve in the temples. There were probably
signs on the temples, which said, CLOSED BECAUSE OF SICKNESS.

> And the LORD hardened the heart of Pharaoh, and he
> hearkened not unto them; as the LORD had spoken unto
> Moses.

> And the LORD said unto Moses, Rise up early in the
> morning, and stand before Pharaoh, and say unto him,
> Thus saith the LORD God of the Hebrews, Let my people
> go, that they may serve me [Exod. 9:12–13].

Even though Pharaoh himself is afflicted with boils, God continues to
ask for the release of His people through His servant Moses. How
many times have we read, "Let my people go that they may serve
me"? How many times have we read God's request, "Let my people
go"? Still Pharaoh refuses to let Israel leave the land. His heart is hard.

> For I will at this time send all my plagues upon thine
> heart, and upon thy servants, and upon thy people; that
> thou mayest know that there is none like me in all the
> earth.

> For now I will stretch out my hand, that I may smite thee
> and thy people with pestilence; and thou shalt be cut off
> from the earth.

And in very deed for this cause have I raised thee up, for
to shew in thee my power; and that my name may be
declared throughout all the earth.

As yet exaltest thou thyself against my people, that thou
wilt not let them go? [Exod. 9:14–17].

God is going to use Pharaoh to demonstrate His power throughout all
of the earth. Here is a case of God using the wrath of man to praise
Him. Psalm 76:10 says, "Surely the wrath of man shall praise
thee. . . ."

THE SEVENTH PLAGUE—HAIL

Behold, to-morrow about this time I will cause it to rain
a very grievous hail, such as hath not been in Egypt
since the foundation thereof even until now [Exod. 9:18].

Egypt is essentially a land of little rain. The average is less than an
inch in one year. God tells them that they are going to have rain—but a
kind they can do without.

Send therefore now, and gather thy cattle, and all that
thou hast in the field; for upon every man and beast
which shall be found in the field, and shall not be
brought home, the hail shall come down upon them,
and they shall die.

He that feared the word of the LORD among the servants
of Pharaoh made his servants and his cattle flee into the
houses [Exod. 9:19–20].

This is a question of whether or not they believed God. God said, "Get
yourselves and your cattle inside." Many people did not believe the
words of God, and they suffered from the judgment. God gave them a
chance, but it was their choice whether or not they believed what He
said. The same holds true today.

And he that regarded not the word of the LORD left his servants and his cattle in the field [Exod. 9:21].

This plague was directed against Isis (sometimes represented as cow-headed), goddess of fertility and considered the goddess of the air. She is the mythical daughter of Set and Nut, the sister and wife of Osiris, and the mother of Horus. It is said that the tears of Isis falling into the Nile River caused it to overflow its banks and bring nourishment to the land. Isis was a prominent goddess in Egypt, and the plague of hail was directed against her.

It is important to note that this plague touches mankind, as well as the animals.

And the LORD said unto Moses, Stretch forth thine hand toward heaven, that there may be hail in all the land of Egypt, upon man, and upon beast, and upon every herb of the field, throughout the land of Egypt.

And Moses stretched forth his rod toward heaven: and the LORD sent thunder and hail, and the fire ran along upon the ground; and the LORD rained hail upon the land of Egypt.

So there was hail, and fire mingled with the hail, very grievous, such as there was none like it in all the land of Egypt since it became a nation.

And the hail smote throughout all the land of Egypt all that was in the field, both man and beast; and the hail smote every herb of the field, and brake every tree of the field [Exod. 9:22–25].

Those who did not believe God made no provision for protection. The message God gave to the Egyptians is the same one He gives to the world today. Judgment is coming. Man is not wise to go on as if nothing is going to happen. It was that way in the days of Noah, and it will be that way when Christ comes again in judgment. Many people in

Egypt did not believe God, and they paid the price for their unbelief. All God asks is that you believe Him.

Only in the land of Goshen, where the children of Israel were, was there no hail [Exod. 9:26].

The land of Goshen is spared from the plagues coming upon the land of Egypt.

And Pharaoh sent, and called for Moses and Aaron, and said unto them, I have sinned this time: the LORD is righteous, and I and my people are wicked [Exod. 9:27].

This is the first time that Pharaoh has made any admission of sin.

And the flax and the barley was smitten: for the barley was in the ear, and the flax was bolled [Exod. 9:31].

The wheat and rye were not smitten in the same way, verse 32 tells us, because they were not yet grown up. It was all beaten down. This was a judgment against the Egyptian food and clothing.

And the heart of Pharaoh was hardened, neither would he let the children of Israel go; as the LORD had spoken by Moses [Exod. 9:35].

God is striking at the Egyptians in an attempt to wake them up and shake them out of their false worship. Pharaoh, leader of the people, continues to harden his heart.

CHAPTER 10

THEME: *Pharaoh is threatened with a plague of locusts; the eighth plague—locusts; the ninth plague —darkness; the Lord's claim on Israel*

PHARAOH IS THREATENED WITH
A PLAGUE OF LOCUSTS

A person begins to wonder what it is going to take to cause Pharaoh to let Israel go.

And the Lord said unto Moses, Go in unto Pharaoh: for I have hardened his heart, and the heart of his servants, that I might shew these my signs before him:

And that thou mayest tell in the ears of thy son, and of thy son's son, what things I have wrought in Egypt, and my signs which I have done among them; that ye may know how that I am the Lord [Exod. 10:1–2].

God has many reasons for doing what He does. One reason for the plagues was to make Pharaoh reveal that he was a godless man. God could have taken the children of Israel out of the land immediately without making any contact with Pharaoh. If He had, the critic would say that God certainly was not fair to Pharaoh. He should have given him an opportunity to let Israel go, and He should have given him an opportunity for salvation. Well, friend, that is exactly what God has done. God also wanted to demonstrate to His people what He was able to do before He took them into the wilderness. He wanted them to know that He was well able to bring them into the land promised to Abraham, Isaac, and Jacob. That story has been told through the observance of the Passover for nearly four thousand years.

And Moses and Aaron came in unto Pharaoh, and said unto him, Thus saith the LORD God of the Hebrews, How long wilt thou refuse to humble thyself before me? let my people go, that they may serve me.

Else, if thou refuse to let my people go, behold, tomorrow will I bring the locusts into thy coast:

And they shall cover the face of the earth, that one cannot be able to see the earth: and they shall eat the residue of that which is escaped, which remaineth unto you from the hail, and shall eat every tree which groweth for you out of the field:

And they shall fill thy houses, and the houses of all thy servants, and the houses of all the Egyptians; which neither thy fathers, nor thy fathers' fathers have seen, since the day that they were upon the earth unto this day. And he turned himself, and went out from Pharaoh.

And Pharaoh's servants said unto him, How long shall this man be a snare unto us? let the men go, that they may serve the LORD their God: knowest thou not yet that Egypt is destroyed? [Exod. 10:3-7].

Pharaoh's servants try to reason with him, "Don't you realize that Egypt is destroyed? How much longer are you going to permit it? Let them go!" So, once again, Moses and Aaron are brought into the presence of Pharaoh.

THE EIGHTH PLAGUE—LOCUSTS

And Moses and Aaron were brought again unto Pharaoh: and he said unto them, Go, serve the LORD your God: but who are they that shall go?

And Moses said, We will go with our young and with our old, with our sons and with our daughters, with our

**flocks and with our herds will we go; for we must hold a
feast unto the LORD.**

**And he said unto them, Let the LORD be so with you, as I
will let you go, and your little ones: look to it: for evil is
before you [Exod. 10:8–10].**

Pharaoh is very angry that they would not accept his compromise.

**Not so: go now ye that are men, and serve the LORD: for
that ye did desire. And they were driven out from Pharaoh's presence [Exod. 10:11].**

Pharaoh told Moses that the adults could go into the wilderness and
sacrifice but they were to go without the children. Pharaoh suspected,
undoubtedly, that if Israel would go three days' journey into the
wilderness they would keep going. He wants to stop them, and he
knows that if he keeps the children, the adults will come back.

Just as Pharaoh tempted and tested Moses with compromise, so
the child of God today is tempted with compromise. Children all
across the country are being brought up in an educational system that
is absolutely contrary to the teachings of Christianity. The child of
God is told that he must learn to get along in the world, make all the
money he can, and get involved in the world. I have been a pastor for
over thirty years, and again and again I have seen Christian parents
want the best for their children. They want them to have the best education. They want them to succeed and be rich. One after another has
fallen and departed from the Lord. Many members of churches I have
served have lost their children to the world. Wanting the "best" of the
world for their children is the most subtle temptation that can come to
Christian parents.

What do you expect, my friends, when you send your children to
these worldly institutions and they come home thoroughly brain-
washed? Why do you say, "My, how could he do that when he was
brought up in a Christian home?" The problem is that he was not actually raised in a Christian home. The parents of many young people

may be lovely Christian people but they did not really train their children in Christian precepts and values. They were so anxious and ambitious for them to get on in the world that they lost them.

Moses and Aaron would *not* accept Pharaoh's compromise, and this made him angry. His anger did not accomplish a thing, however, because another plague was about to begin.

> And the LORD said unto Moses, Stretch out thine hand over the land of Egypt for the locusts, that they may come up upon the land of Egypt, and eat every herb of the land, even all that the hail hath left.
>
> And Moses stretched forth his rod over the land of Egypt, and the LORD brought an east wind upon the land all that day, and all that night; and when it was morning, the east wind brought the locusts.
>
> And the locusts went up over all the land of Egypt, and rested in all the coasts of Egypt: very grievous were they; before them there were no such locusts as they, neither after them shall be such.
>
> For they covered the face of the whole earth, so that the land was darkened; and they did eat every herb of the land, and all the fruit of the trees which the hail had left: and there remained not any green thing in the trees, or in the herbs of the field, through all the land of Egypt [Exod. 10:12–15].

There are several interesting things revealed in this judgment of locusts. Notice that they did not appear miraculously, as did some of the other plagues. An east wind brought them from another place, possibly from somewhere in Asia. Locusts were prominent in the Asian area and this wind had brought them over a broad expanse of desert, and they were pretty hungry when they arrived in the green Nile Valley. They absolutely stripped the land of vegetation.

The locust is used in Scripture as a picture of judgment. A plague of locusts is probably one of the worst things man has to face. The prophet Joel described a plague of locusts in the past, which is a matter of history, then predicted a judgment that is yet in the future for mankind. The Book of Revelation also mentions a great plague of locusts that will come upon the earth. These insects probably had a greater effect upon the land of Egypt than any of the previous plagues that had come upon the land.

> **Then Pharaoh called for Moses and Aaron in haste; and he said, I have sinned against the LORD your God, and against you [Exod. 10:16].**

This is another time Pharaoh has made an admission of sin.

> **Now therefore forgive, I pray thee, my sin only this once, and entreat the LORD your God, that he may take away from me this death only.**

> **And he went out from Pharaoh, and entreated the LORD.**

> **And the LORD turned a mighty strong west wind, which took away the locusts, and cast them into the Red sea; there remained not one locust in all the coasts of Egypt.**

> **But the LORD hardened Pharaoh's heart, so that he would not let the children of Israel go [Exod. 10:17–20].**

There is a method in the way God is dealing with the Egyptians and a systematic and orderly way in which He is sending the plagues. The first plagues were directed against the different gods, goddesses, and idols that infested the land. Now God is beginning to direct the plagues in a manner that works a tremendous hardship upon the people and their struggle to stay alive. The plague of locusts certainly has its effect, and the people try to convince Pharaoh that things are bad. This causes Pharaoh to temporarily repent. The minute the plague is removed, however, Pharaoh changes his mind and goes back to his original position. God is going to force him to let the children of Israel go.

THE NINTH PLAGUE—DARKNESS

And the LORD said unto Moses, Stretch out thine hand toward heaven, that there may be darkness over the land of Egypt, even darkness which may be felt.

And Moses stretched forth his hand toward heaven; and there was a thick darkness in all the land of Egypt three days:

They saw not one another, neither rose any from his place for three days: but all the children of Israel had light in their dwellings [Exod. 10:21–23].

Have you ever been in a place where you could feel the darkness? The only time I have actually felt darkness was down in Carlsbad Caverns. Years ago on a tour of the cave they turned out the lights and the group sang "Rock of Ages." It was very effective. I am told they no longer sing this song because of criticism from some unbelievers, but the blackness of the darkness in that cave could be felt. I have never been in darkness like that before or since, and it was this kind of darkness that was over the land of Egypt. The judgment was upon the sun-god Ra. Darkness came over the land of Egypt in the daytime. God moved in with darkness against the chief god that they worshiped. The sun disc is the most familiar symbol the Egyptians used; it is in all of their art. The plague of darkness showed the utter helplessness of Ra. This darkness was a miracle of God, and it caused Pharaoh to propose a fourth compromise. This was the last compromise he made before he allowed the children of Israel to leave the land of Egypt.

THE LORD'S CLAIM ON ISRAEL

And Pharaoh called unto Moses, and said, Go ye, serve the LORD; only let your flocks and your herds be stayed: let your little ones also go with you [Exod. 10:24].

You would think that just leaving their flocks and herds behind would be a compromise that Moses might make for the Israelites. Pharaoh has come a long way in making concessions to Moses, and you would think this one would be agreeable. Once again there is a lesson here for the modern-day Christian. God called Israel to leave Egypt "lock, stock, and barrel." The children were not to be left in Egypt to be raised in their educational system. If we expect to bring our children up in the wisdom of the world and expect them to pour all of their energies into becoming successful, we should also be prepared to lose them to the world. I listened to a mother tell about how she had sent her son to a godless school, and how he was being advanced. She didn't mention to me that he had lost his faith, although he had. He had graduated from this school, was given a high position. I see his name in print many times. Then she came with tears in her eyes to tell me how her son had turned his back upon everything she held sacred. Well, that's the way she started him out. The world is subtle.

There are also many Christians today who leave their "flocks and herds in the land of Egypt." Egypt, by the way, is a picture of the world. Many Christians are faithful in the church, support their pastor, give to the Lord's work and all the rest, but they do business in the land of Egypt. They put their flocks and herds in Egypt above everything else. If they had to make a choice to serve God or make a trip to Egypt for their flocks and herds, you know which direction they would go.

It is interesting that many Christians say, "I serve the Lord on Sunday, but during the week I am out in the cold-hearted business world." Many of these so-called Christians live so much like folk of the world that it is difficult to tell them apart. They live like everyone else in the land of Egypt. I am of the opinion that the rapture of the church will break the hearts of a great many Christians because it will separate them from their investments in the world. They will have to leave their safe-deposit boxes, savings accounts, their stocks and bonds, and real estate. This is what they have given their time and hearts to, and it will cause them great grief to leave them behind.

Notice what Moses says to this compromise. Moses tells Pharaoh that there will be no compromise.

> **And Moses said, Thou must give us also sacrifices and burnt offerings, that we may sacrifice unto the LORD our God.**
>
> **Our cattle also shall go with us: there shall not an hoof be left behind: for thereof must we take to serve the LORD our God; and we know not with what we must serve the LORD, until we come thither.**
>
> **But the LORD hardened Pharaoh's heart, and he would not let them go.**
>
> **And Pharaoh said unto him, Get thee from me, take heed to thyself, see my face no more; for in that day thou seest my face thou shalt die.**
>
> **And Moses said, Thou hast spoken well, I will see thy face again no more [Exod. 10:25–29].**

There would be no compromise.

CHAPTER 11

THEME: The Israelites ask Egyptians for jewels; the firstborn of Egypt are threatened with death

This is the final chapter in this section of the contest with Pharaoh. The death of the firstborn is the final act of judgment upon Egypt before Israel is freed from the yoke of bondage. Pharaoh should have learned by this time that it is futile to enter into conflict with God. God has been longsuffering and forgiving, but He must make Pharaoh understand that it is time for Israel to leave Egypt. All of Egypt was inclined to take Pharaoh's side in this contest with God and He must deliver one final blow upon Egypt in His attempt to teach them the lessons they need to learn.

THE ISRAELITES ASK EGYPTIANS FOR JEWELS

And the LORD said unto Moses, Yet will I bring one plague more upon Pharaoh, and upon Egypt: afterwards he will let you go hence: when he shall let you go, he shall surely thrust you out hence altogether.

Speak now in the ears of the people, and let every man borrow of his neighbour, and every woman of her neighbour, jewels of silver, and jewels of gold.

And the LORD gave the people favour in the sight of the Egyptians. Moreover the man Moses was very great in the land of Egypt, in the sight of Pharaoh's servants, and in the sight of the people [Exod. 11:1–3].

The word "borrow" in this passage simply means to collect back wages. The Israelites had served for years as slaves and had never received any payment for their labor. Now they were going to get their money. They were literally to go to their neighbors and ask for their back wages. The Lord gave the Israelites favor in the eyes of the Egyptians, and they were glad to pay the children of Israel their just payment.

THE FIRSTBORN OF EGYPT
ARE THREATENED WITH DEATH

And Moses said, Thus saith the Lord, About midnight will I go out into the midst of Egypt:

And all the firstborn in the land of Egypt shall die, from the firstborn of Pharaoh that sitteth upon his throne, even unto the firstborn of the maidservant that is behind the mill; and all the firstborn of beasts.

And there shall be a great cry throughout all the land of Egypt, such as there was none like it, nor shall be like it any more.

But against any of the children of Israel shall not a dog move his tongue, against man or beast: that ye may know how that the Lord doth put a difference between the Egyptians and Israel.

And all these thy servants shall come down unto me, and bow down themselves unto me, saying, Get thee out, and all the people that follow thee: and after that I will go out. And he went out from Pharaoh in a great anger.

And the Lord said unto Moses, Pharaoh shall not hearken unto you; that my wonders may be multiplied in the land of Egypt.

And Moses and Aaron did all these wonders before Pharaoh; and the Lord hardened Pharaoh's heart, so that he would not let the children of Israel go out of his land [Exod. 11:4–10].

Now the firstborn of both man and beast belonged to the gods of Egypt. The Lord God will claim the firstfruits of the Egyptian gods. He is going to show that there is a difference between the children of Israel and the Egyptians. The difference did not lie in the death angel which passed over both the lands of Egypt and Goshen. It did not lie in the fact that one race was Jew and one was Gentile. The difference lay in the blood of the lamb put upon the doorpost. Each home protected by the blood would not be touched by the death angel. This was the beginning of the oldest religious holiday of the Jews, the Passover Feast. The Passover is one of the most eloquent portraits of the Lord Jesus Christ found in the Old Testament.

CHAPTER 12

THEME: The beginning of Israel's religious year; institution of the Feast of the Passover; the tenth plague—death of the firstborn; the Israelites are driven out of Egypt

The Feast of the Passover was instituted as a memorial to Israel's deliverance from Egypt and their adoption as Jehovah's nation. The Passover is a festival that laid the foundation of the nation Israel's birth into a new relationship with God.

THE BEGINNING OF ISRAEL'S RELIGIOUS YEAR

Chapter 12 is a high point in the Book of Exodus. Here we find the institution of the Feast of the Passover. It is a picture of that which Paul speaks of in 1 Corinthians 5:7, ". . . For even Christ our passover is sacrificed for us." Christ is in this chapter.

And the Lord spake unto Moses and Aaron in the land of Egypt, saying,

This month shall be unto you the beginning of months: it shall be the first month of the year to you [Exod. 12:1–2].

This chapter brings us to a new division in the Book of Exodus. The first division (chapters 1—11) deals with Moses, the deliverer. Chapters 12—14 deal with the deliverance of Israel. The first was a deliverer, now it's the deliverance. The deliverance is actually not by Moses. The deliverance is first by blood. That's the Passover Feast, the death of the firstborn. Then in chapters 13 and 14, crossing the Red Sea and the destruction of the army of Egypt are by power. God delivered them by blood and by power. And our redemption today is by blood and by power. The blood that the Lord Jesus Christ shed on the Cross paid the penalty for our sins. The power of the Holy Spirit makes it real and effectual in our sinful hearts. Zechariah 4:6 says, ". . . Not by might, nor by power, but by my spirit, saith the LORD of hosts." Redemption is the work of the Lord Jesus on the Cross for us and the work of the Holy Spirit in us.

Verses 1 and 2 of this chapter tell of the birthday of a nation. When Israel entered Egypt, it was as a family. When they made their exit from Egypt, it was as a nation. The interesting point is that God puts the emphasis on the family here because the family comprises the building blocks out of which the nation was made. You remember how Pharaoh forced the Israelites to make bricks without straw. All the time that Israel was in bondage, God made them the bricks of the family for the building of a nation out of the straws of individuals. An old cliché says, "No nation is stronger than the families of that nation."

The zero hour has come for Israel. The countdown begins in this chapter for the exodus of the children of Israel out of Egypt.

INSTITUTION OF THE FEAST OF THE PASSOVER

Speak ye unto all the congregation of Israel, saying, In the tenth day of this month they shall take to them every man a lamb, according to the house of their fathers, a lamb for an house [Exod. 12:3].

There are two points of emphasis in this verse: (1) the blood and (2) the family. The Israelites have become a nation and God is going to deliver them, but He will do it by families and by the individuals in the family. There was to be a lamb in every house. The lamb, of course, speaks of the blood that will be put on the doorpost.

And if the household be too little for the lamb, let him and his neighbour next unto his house take it according to the number of the souls; every man according to his eating shall make your count for the lamb [Exod. 12:4].

This verse does not say anything about the lamb being too little for the household. This would not happen; the lamb is sufficient. It is possible, however, that the household might be too little for the lamb. God is interested in each individual member of the family. Each family was to have a lamb, but what if a man and his wife were childless or had married children who lived apart from them? This couple is then supposed to join with a neighbor who is in the same position and divide the lamb. Each individual in each family is to receive a part of the lamb. The celebration of the Feast of the Passover is to be a personal, private matter. It is redemption for the nation, yes, but it centers in the family. It must be received and accepted by each individual member in the family. The Passover is a family affair.

God is presenting the modus operandi by which He is going to save individuals. No one is saved because he is the member of a nation or a family. Take, for example, the account of the Philippian jailer and the salvation of his household as told in the Book of Acts, chapter 16. His family was not saved because the jailer believed, but because each member of his family made a transaction with the Lamb; each had to partake of the Lamb. That was true here. Every member had to exhibit his faith in this way. ". . . Believe on the Lord Jesus Christ, and thou shalt be saved, and thy house" (Acts 16:31) does not mean that if you believe, your family will be saved. No! Your family will have to believe on the Lord Jesus Christ, and then they will be saved. Each one will have to participate and partake of it in order to come in under the protection and the redemption of the blood that is out on the doorpost of the house.

We have come to a fateful night in the land of Egypt. The final plague is about to descend upon the people. The Israelites in the land of Goshen were spared during the last three plagues, and God's people were delivered from judgment, but they were not redeemed. Now they have to be redeemed and exhibit faith in the blood.

Your lamb shall be without blemish, a male of the first year: ye shall take it out from the sheep, or from the goats:

> And ye shall keep it up until the fourteenth day of the
> same month: and the whole assembly of the congrega-
> tion of Israel shall kill it in the evening [Exod. 12:5–6].

This portion of Scripture is quite interesting. Note that each family
had a lamb. Thousands of lambs must have been slain that evening,
but the sixth verse reads, "Israel shall kill it in the evening." These
many lambs were speaking of another Lamb. God looked at all of these
lambs as that one Lamb, the Lord Jesus Christ, who was the Passover
offered for us. This feast was pointing to the coming of the Lord Jesus
Christ into the world.

> And they shall take of the blood, and strike it on the two
> side posts and on the upper door post of the houses,
> wherein they shall eat it [Exod. 12:7].

The children of Israel were to put the blood of the lamb outside on the
door. Upon seeing the blood, the death angel would pass over the
house. I believe there is a picture given here that will answer a question that is asked many times: What will happen to the little children
of believers at the time of the Rapture? If small children are in the
house when the Lord comes for His own, will He take the Mom and
Dad and leave the little ones behind? This chapter shows us that God
will not leave the young ones behind.

Inside the home the family is eating the lamb, and by faith they are
partaking of Christ. The young children do not know what is taking
place. Will they be left behind in Egypt when Israel goes out from the
land? If a little one has not yet reached the age of accountability, will
he be slain? Oh no, friend, the blood covers everyone in the family.
God will not leave small children behind at the time of the Rapture
any more than He left them behind when the Israelites were redeemed
and left the land of Egypt.

> And they shall eat the flesh in that night, roast with fire,
> and unleavened bread; and with bitter herbs they shall
> eat it [Exod. 12:8].

Each instruction connected with this feast had a specific meaning and message. This verse speaks of the fellowship of the family. The family entered into the celebration of the Passover *together*. I want to make a statement now that will cause some heated reactions. Today, in our very highly organized church programs, we put the juniors in one place, the junior high group in another place, and the senior high group in still another place. Can't you just hear Moses telling the Israelites to take their babies over to the nursery in Pharaoh's palace because that is where he was raised! Then he might tell them to take the juniors over to the volleyball court, and so forth. May I say to you that a lot of the children would have missed out on the Exodus that night. The observance of the Passover was a family affair, and I am afraid that our churches today are guilty of dividing families. Families should be together in church.

When I was a young preacher in Tennessee, I held meetings in many country churches and had the best time of my life. I would start preaching in the evening to families who might have a baby with them. The mother would cradle a restless child in her arms, and I learned to out-talk them. If I can't out-talk a six-month-old child, there is something radically wrong! So I learned to preach above them. Then the baby would go to sleep, and the mother would take it to the back of the church and put the child on a pallet. She would come back and sit with her husband and maybe two or three other children. Mothers would pop up like popcorn all over the assembly and put their children on the pallets and return to sit with their families. This went on night after night.

One member told me about a preacher who had held meetings in the church about a year ago. He told the congregation that he was a greater preacher than the apostle Paul. He paused for a moment after making that statement because he knew the people would question it. "I am a greater preacher than Paul because he preached until midnight and put only one person to sleep. I have not preached for thirty minutes, and I have put a dozen to sleep." On that basis, friends, I too, am a great preacher!

These small country churches were not very well organized, but they produced some wonderful saints of God. I do not have any confi-

dence in the revolutionary crowd storming our campuses today. We
have done it wrong, friends. God's pattern was family centered and we
have departed from this pattern.

We are also told in this verse that they were to eat the flesh of the
lamb roast with fire. Fire speaks of judgment. There must be judgment of sin. They were to eat the lamb with unleavened bread. Leaven
speaks of sin, and unleavened bread speaks of Christ as the One we
are to feed upon. They were also to partake of this meal with bitter
herbs. Although there are different meanings attached to these herbs,
in this context I believe it means that our experience will not always
be sweet after we have received Jesus Christ as Savior. The bitter herbs
go with redemption.

> **Eat not of it raw, nor sodden at all with water, but roast
> with fire; his head with his legs, and with the pur-
> tenance thereof [Exod. 12:9].**

This sacrifice could not be eaten raw because it spoke of the judgment
of sin in human lives, and this requires sacrifice and the fire of judgment. When a person comes to Christ, he comes as a sinner. The sacrifice was not to be soaked with water. This simply means that we must
trust Christ and Him alone. Unfortunately there are many today who
are trusting in water for their salvation. Everything was to be roasted.
It was the judgment of fire.

> **And thus shall ye eat it; with your loins girded, your
> shoes on your feet, and your staff in your hand; and ye
> shall eat it in haste: it is the LORD's passover.**
>
> **For I will pass through the land of Egypt this night, and
> will smite all the firstborn in the land of Egypt, both
> man and beast; and against all the gods of Egypt I will
> execute judgment: I am the LORD [Exod. 12:11–12].**

Friend, when you come to Christ, you should have your loins girded
and be ready to get out of the world and no longer be involved in it. I

do not believe that you can be converted and continue living a sinful life. This does not mean that you will not sin occasionally, but it does mean that you will not make a habit of living in a pattern of sin.

We had a remarkable instance of a woman in Los Angeles who ran a liquor store and was converted to Christ. She called me by phone and said she was getting out of the liquor business. She said, "If you tell me to take a hammer and break every bottle in the store, I will do it." But it was all she had. I told her to sell the business. She sold it and is a wonderful Christian today.

You will get out of "Egypt" if the blood has been put on the doorposts. You are to eat the sacrificial lamb with your loins girt about, ready to go.

God had directed His plagues, one at a time, against the principal gods of Egypt. All of the gods demanded the offering of the firstborn. Now God is turning His guns against all the Egyptian idols.

And the blood shall be to you for a token upon the houses where ye are: and when I see the blood, I will pass over you, and the plague shall not be upon you to destroy you, when I smite the land of Egypt [Exod. 12:13].

The Israelites were not saved because they were the seed of Abraham. If the Egyptians had obeyed God's command, they, too, would have been saved. God said, "When I see the *blood*, I will pass over you." No one was saved because he was doing the best he could, or because he was honest, or because he was a good person. God said, "When I see the *blood*, I will pass over you." They were not to run out of the house during the night and look at the blood; they were to have confidence and faith in it. They were not saved because they went through the ceremony of circumcision, or because they belonged to some church. God said, "When I see the *blood*, I will pass over you." The death angel was not making a survey of the neighborhood. They were not to open a window and tell the death angel how good they were and how much charity work they had done. Any man who put his neck out of a window that night would have died. God said, "When I see the blood, I will pass over you." Nothing needed to be added. Who was saved that night? Those who believed God. Those who had sprinkled the blood upon their doorposts and trusted in it. Although I do not understand it completely, I believe what God says. He tells me that the shed blood of Christ will save me and nothing else will.

God said that when He saw the blood, He would pass over that home. The blood was not some mystic or superstitious sign. A great principle runs all the way through the Word of God that without shedding of blood, there is no remission of sins. In other words, God cannot arbitrarily or big-heartedly shut His eyes to sin and do nothing about it, any more than can a judge today when the guilty are brought before him. The judge should apply the law to the guilty, and the penalty should be paid. Part of our problem in America today is the laxity in law enforcement. But God's law is inexorable in the universe— "The soul that sinneth, it shall die." The death sentence is upon all of us. But God is gracious, and an innocent life may be substituted for the guilty. Up until Christ came, it was a lamb. Then Jesus was ". . . the Lamb of God, which taketh away the sin of the world" (John 1:29). If we receive Christ, we are saved from the judgment that we deserve as sinners.

Now on that night in Egypt, there was the death of the firstborn in every home that was not protected by the blood. The application of the blood on the doorposts and the lintels of the home was an indication of faith, you see. That answers to the appropriation of a personal faith in Christ.

There followed the Passover Feast. In the Book of Leviticus there are instructions given for the Passover and then the Feast of Unleavened Bread, which actually was part of it, but took place after the Passover Feast.

And this day shall be unto you for a memorial; and ye shall keep it a feast to the LORD throughout your generations; ye shall keep it a feast by an ordinance for ever.

Seven days shall ye eat unleavened bread; even the first day ye shall put away leaven out of your houses: for

whosoever eateth leavened bread from the first day until the seventh day, that soul shall be cut off from Israel.

And in the first day there shall be an holy convocation, and in the seventh day there shall be an holy convocation to you; no manner of work shall be done in them, save that which every man must eat, that only may be done of you [Exod. 12:14–16].

Actually, this has nothing to do with the death angel passing over. It has nothing to do with their salvation. This is a feast of fellowship for those within the home. It is a duty, of course—God commanded it— and it is also a privilege. They are to have fellowship with God.

And ye shall observe the feast of unleavened bread; for in this selfsame day have I brought your armies out of the land of Egypt: therefore shall ye observe this day in your generations by an ordinance for ever [Exod. 12:17].

They ate the unleavened bread on the wilderness march because on the night of the Passover they were expelled from Egypt. And they ate the bread for seven days.

Notice that it is unleavened bread. If they ate leavened bread they were cut off—that is, cut off from fellowship.

Leaven is mentioned eight times between verses 14 and 20.

Seven days shall there be no leaven found in your houses: for whosoever eateth that which is leavened, even that soul shall be cut off from the congregation of Israel, whether he be a stranger, or born in the land.

Ye shall eat nothing leavened; in all your habitations shall ye eat unleavened bread [Exod. 12:19–20].

Leaven is a principle of evil. It represents that which is evil and offensive. In the thirteenth chapter of Matthew there is a parable about a woman hiding leaven in three measures of meal. That leaven is not the gospel because leaven is a principle of evil. The three measures of meal represent the Word of God, and leaven (evil) has been put into it. It is amazing to see the amount of error being taught today, and how many gullible folk believe it. "Leaven" is being mixed into the teaching of the Word. All of the cults and "isms" use the Bible, but mix false doctrine with it. This is what the children of Israel were told to avoid.

Our Lord made this matter of "leaven" clear in the Gospel of Matthew. Matthew 16:6 says, "Then Jesus said unto them, Take heed and beware of the leaven of the Pharisees and of the Sadducees." Then Matthew 16:11 continues, "How is it that ye do not understand that I spake it not to you concerning bread, that ye should beware of the leaven of the Pharisees and of the Sadducees?" The Lord's disciples, at this time, thought He was speaking about physical bread. Later they understood that the Lord was speaking about the *doctrine* of the Pharisees, which was evil.

Unleavened bread is not palatable. There are a great many people who do not like the study of the Bible, the pure, unleavened Word of God. Many people love to come to church for the social time, or the music, or the beauty of the place, but not for the Word of God. They do not want the Word of God because it is not palatable to them.

I have been in Israel during the Feast of Unleavened Bread and never got so tired of unleavened bread in my life because I was brought up in the South where we had hot biscuits that puff right up. What a wonderful night it was when this feast came to an end and they brought out the real bread. It tasted good to the natural man. Unleavened bread is not as tasty as the leavened bread is, but the Word of God is the food that is good for the child of God.

> **And ye shall take a bunch of hyssop, and dip it in the blood that is in the basin, and strike the lintel and the two side posts with the blood that is in the basin; and none of you shall go out at the door of his house until the morning.**
>
> **For the LORD will pass through to smite the Egyptians; and when he seeth the blood upon the lintel, and on the**

two side posts, the LORD will pass over the door, and will
not suffer the destroyer to come in unto your houses to
smite you [Exod. 12:22-23].

Have you wondered how they put the blood on the doorposts? Hyssop
is a fluffy little plant that grows around rocks. It was used to apply the
blood to the house. Hyssop, to me, represents faith. That is the way
the blood of Christ is applied to your heart and life. You trust what
Christ has done when He died for you.

THE TENTH PLAGUE—DEATH OF THE FIRSTBORN

This is the last judgment and the last plague to come upon the land
of Egypt. God had prepared His people for it. The land of Goshen had
escaped the last three plagues but could not escape this one unless
there was blood on the doorposts. Any Egyptian could follow the example of the Israelites—put blood on his doorpost and believe God—
and the death angel would have spared the firstborn in his house. It is
going to surprise many people someday when they discover that the
Lord Jesus is not going to ask which church they belonged to. If you
have trusted Christ as your Savior, the Holy Spirit of God has baptized
you into the body of believers, and you are a member of the true
church.

And it came to pass, that at midnight the LORD smote all
the firstborn in the land of Egypt, from the firstborn of
Pharaoh that sat on his throne unto the firstborn of the
captive that was in the dungeon; and all the firstborn of
cattle.

And Pharaoh rose up in the night, he, and all his servants, and all the Egyptians; and there was a great cry
in Egypt; for there was not a house where there was not
one dead [Exod. 12:29-30].

This final judgment claimed the life of the firstborn in each house. Up
to this point God had not touched human life. Now he does, but do not

say that God is a murderer. "The Lord gives and the Lord takes away; blessed be the name of the Lord." He who creates life has the authority to take it away.

THE ISRAELITES ARE DRIVEN OUT OF EGYPT

That night Pharaoh got up:

> And he called for Moses and Aaron by night, and said, Rise up, and get you forth from among my people, both ye and the children of Israel; and go, serve the LORD, as ye have said.

> Also take your flocks and your herds, as ye have said, and be gone; and bless me also [Exod. 12:31–32].

Pharaoh finally has had to give up. Until now he has been reluctant to give in to Moses' demands but this plague reached in and touched his own son. God did not begin by touching the lives of the firstborn; He began the contest with Pharaoh by changing Aaron's rod into a crocodile. If Pharaoh had believed God, the children of Israel could have left the land and he would have spared his people the judgments. The blame, therefore, should not belong to God.

> And the Egyptians were urgent upon the people, that they might send them out of the land in haste; for they said, We be all dead men [Exod. 12:33].

The Egyptians did not know where the judgment of God would end. God had taken their firstborn; what would He do next? Perhaps He would bring death to all the Egyptians, and so Pharaoh and the people told the Israelites to get out of the land because they feared for their own lives.

> And the people took their dough before it was leavened, their kneadingtroughs being bound up in their clothes upon their shoulders.

**And the children of Israel did according to the word
of Moses; and they borrowed of the Egyptians jewels
of silver, and jewels of gold, and raiment [Exod.
12:34–35].**

The word "borrow" is the Hebrew *shaal*, meaning "to ask." God gave
them favor in the sight of the Egyptians so that when they asked, the
Egyptians gave (not lent) them whatever they wanted. It was God's
way of simply collecting back wages for their years of slave labor in
Egypt. The Egyptians owed the Israelites so much in back wages that
the children of Israel spoiled them; that is, Israel left with much of
Egypt's wealth.

**And the children of Israel journeyed from Rameses to
Succoth, about six hundred thousand on foot that were
men, beside children [Exod. 12:37].**

It would seem that there came out of the land of Egypt well over one
million, and perhaps as many as two million people. There were six
hundred thousand men on foot besides all the women and children.
Then our attention is called to another interesting fact:

**And a mixed multitude went up also with them; and
flocks, and herds, even very much cattle [Exod. 12:38].**

In addition to the Israelites that left Egypt, a mixed multitude left with
them. They will be the cause of much trouble in the camp of Israel. We
learn more about them in the Book of Numbers; the mixed multitude
are troublemakers. Factually, they are a mixed race. An Egyptian married a Jewish maiden or a Hebrew married an Egyptian maiden. The
offspring of a union like this had to make a decision—shall he go out
of the land of Egypt with the Israelites or stay with the Egyptians?
Many of the mixed multitude left the land and many stayed. Those
who left often wondered if they had made a mistake, and when trouble
and hardship came they were the first to complain. They were not
Israelites in the true sense of the word.

One of the big problems in Israel today is the mixed multitude, those who have a gentile parent. Are they Israelites? Also we have a problem in the church with those who join the church but are not saved. I have been a pastor for a long time, and I have never believed that a troublemaker in a church is really a child of God. (But let's understand what we mean by troublemakers. We deal with that in Num. 11.)

> And they baked unleavened cakes of the dough which they brought forth out of Egypt, for it was not leavened; because they were thrust out of Egypt, and could not tarry, neither had they prepared for themselves any victual.
>
> Now the sojourning of the children of Israel, who dwelt in Egypt, was four hundred and thirty years.
>
> And it came to pass at the end of the four hundred and thirty years, even the selfsame day it came to pass, that all the hosts of the LORD went out from the land of Egypt.
>
> It is a night to be much observed unto the LORD for bringing them out from the land of Egypt: this is that night of the LORD to be observed of all the children of Israel in their generations [Exod. 12:39–42].

The celebration of the Passover goes back to the exodus of Israel out of the land of Egypt. They were never to forget what the Lord God did for them until the King comes again and the Millennium is established. And then they will forget it. We will see that later.

> All the congregation of Israel shall keep it.
>
> And when a stranger shall sojourn with thee, and will keep the passover to the LORD, let all his males be circumcised, and then let him come near and keep it; and he shall be as one that is born in the land: for no uncircumcised person shall eat thereof [Exod. 12:47–48].

Only those who identified themselves by faith with the people of God could take part in this observance. If a Gentile wanted to identify himself in belief with Israel, he was welcome.

> **One law shall be to him that is homeborn, and unto the stranger that sojourneth among you.**

> **Thus did all the children of Israel; as the LORD commanded Moses and Aaron, so did they.**

> **And it came to pass the selfsame day, that the LORD did bring the children of Israel out of the land of Egypt by their armies [Exod. 12:49-51].**

As we follow the children of Israel out of Egypt, to the Red Sea and into the wilderness, we will learn lessons that correspond to experiences in the Christian life today.

CHAPTER 13

THEME: Israel's firstborn sanctified to God; journey to
Etham by divine guidance

ISRAEL'S FIRSTBORN SANCTIFIED TO GOD

The children of Israel are leaving the land of Egypt and moving
toward the Red Sea.

And the Lord spake unto Moses, saying,

**Sanctify unto me all the firstborn, whatsoever openeth
the womb among the children of Israel, both of man and
of beast: it is mine.**

**And Moses said unto the people, Remember this day, in
which ye came out from Egypt, out of the house of bondage; for by strength of hand the Lord brought you out
from this place: there shall no leavened bread be eaten
[Exod. 13:1–3].**

The firstborn in Egypt had died. The gods of Egypt had always
claimed the firstborn as their own, and now God claims the firstborn
of Israel as His own. He wants the first from believers today, also.
Many Christians do not give Him the first place. God claims our best,
our very best; God claims the first in everything. Even though He
wants first place in our lives, many believers put Him last, and that
creates a problem. If we have time, we work for the Lord, but most of
our time is spent on personal interests and amusements. We usually
give the Lord what is left over.

I remember hearing Billy Sunday tell a story years ago. He was
riding across the country with William Wrigley, the chewing gum
man. Mr. Wrigley was a Christian, and as they rode on the train he
told Billy Sunday that he had made it a practice in his life to give the
Lord one-tenth of everything that he made, and he added that it was

not the last tenth he made that he gave to the Lord. William Wrigley gave the Lord the *first* tenth of his earnings. It is quite interesting how the Lord blessed him and prospered him. Now God doesn't guarantee material prosperity to anyone, but it is interesting how He has blessed men and women who put Him first. And to put Him first means no half truth in *saying* we put Him first—no compromising.

The children of Israel have just come out of Egypt where they served for years as slaves. Then God immediately requires of them their firstborn. Many of them probably said, "Look, Lord, you have just delivered us out of slavery and now you are claiming our firstborn for your own!" The Lord Jesus Christ does the same thing for you and me. He saves us out of the bondage of sin, delivers us, and sets us free. God says, "If the Son therefore shall make you free, ye shall be free indeed" (John 8:36). The Lord is also saying that He wants us to give ourselves to Him. You say, "I'm free!" Are you really free? You have been bought with a price—the precious blood of Jesus Christ. The blessing comes when you give yourself to Him voluntarily and put Him first.

> **And it shall be when the LORD shall bring thee into the land of the Canaanites, and the Hittites, and the Amorites, and the Hivites, and the Jebusites, which he sware unto thy fathers to give thee, a land flowing with milk and honey, that thou shalt keep this service in this month [Exod. 13:5].**

In other words, the Israelites were to observe the Passover Feast and the Feast of Unleavened Bread.

> **Seven days thou shalt eat unleavened bread, and in the seventh day shall be a feast to the LORD.**

> **Unleavened bread shall be eaten seven days; and there shall no leavened bread be seen with thee, neither shall there be leaven seen with thee in all thy quarters [Exod. 13:6–7].**

When the Israelites left Egypt, they took on their journey their kneading troughs and the dough that was in them. This was unleavened dough and God says, "I want you to get rid of leaven. Unleavened bread shall be eaten seven days, and there shall no leavened
bread be seen with thee nor in thy house."

> And thou shalt shew thy son in that day, saying, This is
> done because of that which the LORD did unto me when I
> came forth out of Egypt [Exod. 13:8].

This observance was to be passed from one generation to the other so
that the people would always remember that God delivered them out
of the land of Egypt.

> And it shall be for a sign unto thee upon thine hand, and
> for a memorial between thine eyes, that the LORD's law
> may be in thy mouth: for with a strong hand hath the
> LORD brought thee out of Egypt.

> Thou shalt therefore keep this ordinance in his season
> from year to year.

> And it shall be when the LORD shall bring thee into the
> land of the Canaanites, as he sware unto thee and to thy
> fathers, and shall give it thee,

> That thou shalt set apart unto the LORD all that openeth
> the matrix, and every firstling that cometh of a beast
> which thou hast; the males shall be the LORD's [Exod.
> 13:9–12].

The firstborn of all the stock that belonged to the children of Israel
belonged to the Lord.

> And every firstling of an ass thou shalt redeem with a
> lamb; and if thou wilt not redeem it, then thou shalt
> break his neck: and all the firstborn of man among thy
> children shalt thou redeem [Exod. 13:13].

Every firstling of an ass was to be redeemed with a lamb. God did not
want one of these long-eared animals as an offering. The offering had
to be a lamb. The firstborn of man among their children were to be
redeemed, as we shall see later on, by silver. Silver was the redemption money.

> **And it shall be when thy son asketh thee in time to
> come, saying, What is this? that thou shalt say unto him,
> By strength of hand the LORD brought us out from Egypt,
> from the house of bondage:**
>
> **And it came to pass, when Pharaoh would hardly let us
> go, that the LORD slew all the firstborn in the land of
> Egypt, both the firstborn of man, and the firstborn of
> beast: therefore I sacrifice to the LORD all that openeth
> the matrix, being males; but all the firstborn of my chil-
> dren I redeem [Exod. 13:14–15].**

This observance was to remind the Israelites that God delivered them
out of the land of Egypt. The firstborn of their sons had to be redeemed by silver. We are told in 1 Peter 1:18–19 that, "Forasmuch as
ye know that ye were not redeemed with corruptible things, as silver
and gold, from your vain conversation received by tradition from your
fathers; but with the precious blood of Christ, as of a lamb without
blemish and without spot."

> **And it came to pass, when Pharaoh had let the people
> go, that God led them not through the way of the land of
> the Philistines, although that was near; for God said,
> Lest peradventure the people repent when they see war,
> and they return to Egypt [Exod. 13:17].**

The Israelites had just come out of slavery, and they were not prepared
for warfare. The shortest way for them to go to the land which God had
given them was up the sea coast. During the 1967 Six-Day War in the

land of Palestine, the Israelites moved right down the sea coast and moved the Egyptians right out. Of course, the Israelites had tanks and planes to do it. They were prepared. The Israelites coming out of Egyptian slavery had no weapons to fight with; so God graciously took them through the wilderness. It was a longer route to the land, but it would spare any warfare. They would not have to face an enemy until they entered the land. It took them forty years to get through the wilderness and into the Promised Land. By then they would have an army and be equipped, as we shall see.

Someone might say, "But God could have delivered them by some miracle." This is true, but this kind of an attitude makes me sick. Some Christians think that God should perform a miracle for them every minute. They feel that they have the right to command the Lord to intervene for them if they are sick or in trouble. It is not a question of His ability; He certainly can do it. Rather, it is a question of the *way* God wants to do it. He is following a plan. And when it is necessary, God will perform a miracle for us—but only to accomplish His will and way in our lives.

God could have brought the Israelites through the land of the Philistines by a miracle. Had they been attacked, God could have delivered them. When it is necessary, God is prepared to perform miracles but only to accomplish His will.

But God led the people about, through the way of the wilderness of the Red sea: and the children of Israel went up harnessed out of the land of Egypt [Exod. 13:18].

The word "harnessed" is an interesting word. It means that the children of Israel left Egypt in an orderly manner. They did not come out of the land like a mob but in an organized way. They did not have an army but they lined up five in a row. If you had seen them going through the wilderness, you would have observed a most orderly group.

And Moses took the bones of Joseph with him: for he had
straitly sworn the children of Israel, saying, God will
surely visit you; and ye shall carry up my bones away
hence with you [Exod. 13:19].

When the Israelites left Egypt, Moses took the bones of Joseph. There
is an interesting passage in Genesis 50:24 which says, "And Joseph
said unto his brethren, I die: and God will surely visit you, and bring
you out of this land unto the land which he sware to Abraham, to
Isaac, and to Jacob." Genesis 50:25 continues by saying, "And Joseph
took an oath of the children of Israel, saying, God will surely visit you,
and ye shall carry up my bones from hence." At least two hundred
years had elapsed since Joseph had spoken these words, but now the
time had come. When he died, he was a national hero and would have
to be buried in Egypt. But eventually a Pharaoh arose who did not
know Joseph. Since Joseph was no longer a national hero, his bones
could be removed from Egypt without protest.

Joseph wanted to be buried in the Promised Land. But why remove
his body and bury it in the land? If Joseph knew he would be raised
from the dead someday and taken up to heaven, what difference
would it make if his launching pad was in Egypt or in the land of
Israel? Well, the fact of the matter is that he was not expecting to go to
heaven. He expected to be raised in the resurrection of his people in
that land for the Millennium—and then for eternity. This will be
heaven for them. This was the hope of Joseph, and it is also the hope of
Moses. By faith Moses takes the bones of Joseph to the Promised Land.

JOURNEY TO ETHAM BY DIVINE GUIDANCE

And they took their journey from Succoth, and encamped in Etham, in the edge of the wilderness.

And the LORD went before them by day in a pillar of a
cloud, to lead them the way; and by night in a pillar of
fire, to give them light; to go by day and night:

He took not away the pillar of the cloud by day, nor the pillar of fire by night, from before the people [Exod. 13:20-22].

The children of Israel are moving toward the hot, burning desert that even Moses called a great and terrible wilderness. They went through it and did not even get sunburned because they had a pillar of cloud over them by day. This nation had something that no other nation has ever had: the Glory, the visible presence of God. When Paul was defining his kinsman, he said, "Who are Israelites; to whom pertaineth the adoption, and the glory . . ." (Rom. 9:4). These people had the glory, the visible presence of God.

Not even the church has the visible presence of God with it. Nothing visible has been given to the church. Ephesians 1:3 tells us that God ". . . hath blessed us with all *spiritual* blessings in heavenly places in Christ." They were looking forward to the coming of Christ, and *we* look back to an historical event. We do not need the visible presence of God in order to walk by faith. They needed the "glory" because the redemption had not yet been worked out in history as it has now.

God made every preparation for every eventuality in order to bring His people safely through the wilderness.

CHAPTER 14

THEME: Pharaoh and his army pursue Israel; God's victory over Egypt

PHARAOH AND HIS ARMY PURSUE ISRAEL

And the LORD spake unto Moses, saying,

Speak unto the children of Israel, that they turn and encamp before Pi-hahiroth, between Migdol and the sea, over against Baal-zephon: before it shall ye encamp by the sea [Exod. 14:1-2].

It is impossible to locate these places definitely, but they were somewhere between the Nile River and the Red Sea.

For Pharaoh will say of the children of Israel, They are entangled in the land, the wilderness hath shut them in [Exod. 14:3].

Pharaoh has spies watching the children of Israel. The movement of perhaps two and a half million people would be difficult to conceal anyway. Pharaoh expects the Israelites to move up the coastal route and through the land of the Philistines. When they head toward the wilderness, he thinks they are lost and do not know where they are going. God says that when he thinks they are trapped, he will pursue them. It is obvious that Pharaoh let the Israelites go reluctantly. God is not through with this man Pharaoh yet.

And I will harden Pharaoh's heart, that he shall follow after them; and I will be honoured upon Pharaoh, and upon all his host; that the Egyptians may know that I am the LORD. And they did so [Exod. 14:4].

You would think that the Egyptians had experienced enough disaster, but something even more profound is going to take place that will convince them.

> **And it was told the king of Egypt that the people fled: and the heart of Pharaoh and of his servants was turned against the people, and they said, Why have we done this, that we have let Israel go from serving us?**
>
> **And he made ready his chariot, and took his people with him:**
>
> **And he took six hundred chosen chariots, and all the chariots of Egypt, and captains over every one of them [Exod. 14:5-7].**

The host of Egypt moves against the children of Israel with six hundred chariots. You can imagine what that number of chariots could do to a poor, helpless, defenseless people—especially women, children and cattle. They would make havoc and hash of them!

> **And the LORD hardened the heart of Pharaoh king of Egypt, and he pursued after the children of Israel: and the children of Israel went out with an high hand.**
>
> **But the Egyptians pursued after them, all the horses and chariots of Pharaoh, and his horsemen, and his army, and overtook them encamping by the sea, beside Pi-hahiroth, before Baal-zephon.**
>
> **And when Pharaoh drew nigh, the children of Israel lifted up their eyes, and, behold, the Egyptians marched after them; and they were sore afraid: and the children of Israel cried out unto the LORD [Exod. 14:8-10].**

The Red Sea is ahead of the Israelites, and the hosts of Egypt are behind them. These poor defenseless people are caught between the

Devil and the deep blue sea. From a natural viewpoint, the Israelites
are in a bad spot.

> **And they said unto Moses, Because there were no graves
> in Egypt, hast thou taken us away to die in the wilder-
> ness? wherefore hast thou dealt thus with us, to carry us
> forth out of Egypt? [Exod. 14:11].**

This is a rather ironic statement, and I am sure it was even more so in
that day. The great pyramids stood as monuments to the burial places
of kings. Mummies were all over the place in Egypt; it was a great
burying ground. The children of Israel were saying, "Did you bring us
all the way out into the wilderness to die because there was not room
to bury us in the land of Egypt?" The Israelites are sure they are going
to be slaughtered out in the wilderness.

> **Is not this the word that we did tell thee in Egypt, say-
> ing, Let us alone, that we may serve the Egyptians? For it
> had been better for us to serve the Egyptians, than that
> we should die in the wilderness [Exod. 14:12].**

The Israelites, when they were in the land of Egypt, cried out for deliverance. God provided the opportunity for them to leave; but the
minute they were in danger, they wanted to return to Egypt.

Now notice what God is going to do for His people. They are helpless and hopeless without the aid of God. If they are to be redeemed,
God will have to do it. I wish we could get that objective viewpoint of
ourselves today because we are just like the Israelites. If we could go
with the astronauts to the moon and look down on this little earth of
ours, we would see people lost in sin. Actually our world is a pretty
hopeless place; a great burying ground. In Romans 5:12 Paul tells us,
"Wherefore, as by one man sin entered into the world, and death by
sin; and so death passed upon all men, for that all have sinned." Man
has been on the march for over five thousand years. Where is he
marching to? Man is marching to the grave. It isn't pretty, but it is
true. Man is the most colossal failure in God's universe.

GOD'S VICTORY OVER EGYPT

Look at these children of Israel. Unless God moves on their behalf, they are doomed. And you and I could never be redeemed unless God did it, friends. Redemption is the work of the Lord. Jonah said, ". . . Salvation is of the Lord" (Jonah 2:9); King David made the same statement, and that is the message of the New Testament.

And Moses said unto the people, Fear ye not, stand still, and see the salvation of the Lord, which he will shew to you to-day: for the Egyptians whom ye have seen to-day, ye shall see them again no more for ever [Exod. 14:13].

The Lord will work in behalf of His people; all they have to do is accept and receive His salvation. They are to stand still and God will do the work. Remember, you cannot lift a little finger to work out your salvation. All you have to do is accept what God has done for you.

The Lord shall fight for you, and ye shall hold your peace [Exod. 14:14].

God will bring salvation to His people and will bring the peace that comes from having sins forgiven.

And the Lord said unto Moses, Wherefore criest thou unto me? speak unto the children of Israel, that they go forward:

But lift thou up thy rod, and stretch out thine hand over the sea, and divide it: and the children of Israel shall go on dry ground through the midst of the sea [Exod. 14:15-16].

The Israelites are to stand still and see the salvation of the Lord. But when it is wrought they are to lay hold of His instructions by faith. Their faith will be evidenced in whether or not they will go forward.

Many natural explanations are offered as to how the children of Israel crossed the sea. First, I believe it is well established by reputable, conservative historians and theologians that the exodus of Israel is a historical fact. The problem for most people comes in trying to figure out *how* they crossed the Red Sea. Some say that the wind blew the water back. But there was a wall of water on both sides of the path. Others say that some sort of a natural phenomenon rolled back the sea. Still others claim that an earthquake took place at the exact moment they were ready to cross the sea. The thing that must be faced here is that a miracle took place. You either accept it or you do not. God, by a miracle, opened the sea and the Israelites walked through it on dry ground.

When the Israelites crossed the sea, they crossed to the other side dry-shod. There was not even enough water for them to get their feet damp. It would be difficult to explain this apart from a direct miracle.

And I, behold, I will harden the hearts of the Egyptians, and they shall follow them: and I will get me honour upon Pharaoh, and upon all his host, upon his chariots, and upon his horsemen [Exod. 14:17].

Had you been at the water's edge when Pharaoh started to follow the children of Israel across the Red Sea, you would have said to him, "I suppose that you recognize that you are doing this because your heart and the hearts of your people are hardened by God, and you really don't want to do it." I think Pharaoh and his army would have laughed at you and replied, "We are chasing the Israelites because we want to." The fact is that God is forcing the Egyptians to do the thing that is in their hearts.

And the Egyptians shall know that I am the LORD, when I have gotten me honour upon Pharaoh, upon his chariots, and upon his horsemen.

And the angel of God, which went before the camp of Israel, removed and went behind them; and the pillar of

the cloud went from before their face, and stood behind them:

And it came between the camp of the Egyptians and the camp of Israel; and it was a cloud and darkness to them, but it gave light by night to these: so that the one came not near the other all the night.

And Moses stretched out his hand over the sea; and the LORD caused the sea to go back by a strong east wind all that night, and made the sea dry land, and the waters were divided [Exod. 14:18–21].

There are several things to take note of in this passage. First of all, the Egyptians mentioned in verse 18 are the people who are left back in the land of Egypt. Israel will cross safely to the other side of the Red Sea, and Pharaoh and his army will perish in the waters of that sea, and the Egyptians left in the land will know that the God of the Israelites is the Lord. In verse 19 the "angel of God" is mentioned. I believe the Angel of God was none other than the pre-incarnate Christ. It was God Himself who stood between the Egyptians and the Israelites. When a strong east wind came, it caused the sea to go back. A natural wind could never have made a wall of water on both sides.

And the children of Israel went into the midst of the sea upon the dry ground: and the waters were a wall unto them on their right hand, and on their left.

And the Egyptians pursued, and went in after them to the midst of the sea, even all Pharaoh's horses, his chariots, and his horsemen.

And it came to pass, that in the morning watch the LORD looked unto the host of the Egyptians through the pillar of fire and of the cloud, and troubled the host of the Egyptians,

> And took off their chariot wheels, that they drove them
> heavily: so that the Egyptians said, Let us flee from the
> face of Israel; for the LORD fighteth for them against the
> Egyptians [Exod. 14:22–25].

As God works out His plan to deliver His people, once again we see that He worked through the pillar of fire and the cloud, which I believe represent the Holy Spirit. They were led, as the child of God should be led today, by the Spirit of God.

It becomes clear to the Egyptians that what is happening to them is certainly supernatural. They want to retreat and escape the forces which are against them.

> And the LORD said unto Moses, Stretch out thine hand
> over the sea, that the waters may come again upon the
> Egyptians, upon their chariots, and upon their horse-
> men.
>
> And Moses stretched forth his hand over the sea, and
> the sea returned to his strength when the morning ap-
> peared; and the Egyptians fled against it; and the LORD
> overthrew the Egyptians in the midst of the sea.
>
> And the waters returned, and covered the chariots, and
> the horsemen, and all the host of Pharaoh that came into
> the sea after them; there remained not so much as one of
> them [Exod. 14:26–28].

This account needs close observation because it is a *miracle*. There is no natural way to explain what happened. Many conservative men, although they believe in the Word of God and are saved by faith alone in Christ, try to explain the crossing of the Red Sea in some natural way. When you read this record, it is impossible to explain it naturally. God says it is a miracle and you either take it or leave it.

But the children of Israel walked upon dry land in the
midst of the sea; and the waters were a wall unto them
on their right hand, and on their left [Exod. 14:29].

This is a miracle. Twice, now, this has been made clear to us. They
walked on dry land through the midst of the sea. The waters were a
wall to them on the left side and on the right side. You cannot explain
it on a natural basis.

Thus the LORD saved Israel that day out of the hand of
the Egyptians; and Israel saw the Egyptians dead upon
the sea shore.

And Israel saw that great work which the LORD did upon
the Egyptians: and the people feared the LORD, and
believed the LORD, and his servant Moses [Exod.
14:30–31].

These two verses state the purpose for God's deliverance of Israel. At
the beginning of their wilderness march they saw the power of God
when He delivered them by blood out of Egypt. Now at the Red Sea He
demonstrates His power again by taking them safely across the sea
and by destroying the Egyptians pursuing them. God delivers His
children by power.

CHAPTER 15

THEME: Israel's song of redemption; Israel murmurs because they lack water

ISRAEL'S SONG OF REDEMPTION

Immediately upon their safe journey across the Red Sea, the children of Israel join in singing a song.

> Then sang Moses and the children of Israel this song unto the Lord, and spake, saying, I will sing unto the Lord, for he hath triumphed gloriously: the horse and his rider hath he thrown into the sea.
>
> The Lord is my strength and song, and he is become my salvation: he is my God, and I will prepare him an habitation; my father's God, and I will exalt him.
>
> The Lord is a man of war: the Lord is his name [Exod. 15:1–3].

They are singing lustily now. This is the same crowd, friends, that only a few hours before on the other side of the Red Sea were moaning, crying out that they wanted to go back to Egypt and saying, "Because there were no graves in Egypt, hast thou taken us away to die in the wilderness?" We are told in 1 Corinthians 10:11 that, ". . . all these things happened unto them for ensamples: and they are written for our admonition, upon whom the ends of the world are come." God uses this experience to teach us a very important truth. "Moreover, brethren, I would not that ye should be ignorant, how that all our fathers were under the cloud, and all passed through the sea; and were all baptized unto Moses in the cloud and in the sea" (1 Cor. 10:1–2). How were the children of Israel baptized unto Moses? It could not have been by water because they crossed the sea dry-shod.

Not a drop of water fell upon them. If you want to talk about water, take a good look at the Egyptians; they were the ones who got wet. Then what does it mean that the Israelites were baptized unto Moses in the cloud and in the sea? It means that they were identified. The primary meaning of *baptism* is identification. The ritual of baptism is the baptism of water, and I believe it is important. It sets forth the real baptism which is of the Holy Spirit and identifies us with Christ and puts us in Christ. Now how were the Israelites baptized unto Moses? They complained on one side of the sea, and when they crossed to the other side, they sang the song of Moses. They were identified with Moses. They were delivered through him.

"By faith they passed through the Red sea as by dry land: which the Egyptians assaying to do were drowned" (Heb. 11:29). It was "by faith" that the Israelites crossed the sea. Whose faith was it? It was not the faith of the children of Israel because they did not have any until they crossed over the sea. They were identified with Moses. It was Moses' faith. It was Moses who smote the Red Sea. It was Moses who led them across. When they reached the other side of the sea, it was Moses who lifted the song of deliverance. Now they have seen the salvation of God. They are identified with Moses. They have been baptized unto Moses.

Friends, this is what happens when you trust the Lord Jesus Christ as Savior. He is the One who takes us out of the Egyptian bondage and the Egyptian darkness of this world. He leads us across the Red Sea. It is His deliverance and His salvation and His redemption. He brings us to the place where we can lift a song of redemption unto Him. Then we are joined to Him. We are baptized into Christ. First Corinthians 12:13 says, "For by one Spirit are we all baptized into one body, whether we be Jews or Gentiles, whether we be bond or free; and have been all made to drink into one Spirit." The Holy Spirit is the one who joins us to Christ and causes us to become one with Him. It is a wonderful thing to be joined to Him!

A dear little lady talking about the assurance of her salvation once said, "Nobody can take you out of His hand." Someone replied, "Well, you might slip through His fingers." And she replied, "Oh my no, I couldn't slip through His fingers; I am one of His fingers." That is true, friends. We are members of the body of Christ. The Holy Spirit of God joins us to Him. What a wonderful redemption we have in Christ! What happened to Israel is an example for us. It is a picture of our redemption and what the Spirit of God does when we trust the Lord Jesus Christ as Savior.

Before the Israelites joined in with Moses to sing to their God the song of redemption, they were singing the blues, the Desert Blues. Before they crossed the sea, they sang the blues loud and long, and they will be returning to the Desert Blues again because it will be their theme song as they travel through the desert. For a time, however, they lustily sang the song of redemption.

This song can be compared with the song of Deborah and Barak in the Book of Judges. There are many songs in the Bible. David composed and sang many songs found in the Psalms. You will find that his songs are great songs. Even Jeremiah had a song, even though it was often with a wail. Other prophets had songs throughout the Old Testament.

The New Testament opens with songs. Dr. Luke records several of them. There is the song of Elizabeth when word was brought to her that she was to have a child. Mary sang a song when she learned she was to be the mother of the Lord Jesus Christ. Other great songs were connected with the birth of Christ. Finally in the Book of Revelation we get a glimpse into heaven as we see a great company gathered around the throne of God singing a new song. Probably that is going to be the first time I will be able to sing. Up to the present time I don't do very well, but by that time—with a new body and a new voice—I am sure I will be able to sing a new song.

With all the talk about peace today it might be well for everyone to read this song of Moses. It tells us that Jehovah is a man of war. In the nineteenth chapter of Revelation we see Him coming to earth and putting down all unrighteousness. Until He does that, the earth will never have peace. In Matthew 10:34 the Lord said, "Think not that I am come to send peace on earth: I came not to send peace, but a sword." These words were spoken about His first coming to the earth. The second time He comes to earth He will bring peace with the sword. That is the only way to rid the earth of unrighteousness.

This song of Moses and the Israelites recounts the wonderful experience they had in crossing the Red Sea. Their song told the story of what they had seen God do and of what God had done for them. It was something they were not apt to forget, but this song certainly kept the experience before them.

> **Pharaoh's chariots and his host hath he cast into the sea: his chosen captains also are drowned in the Red sea.**
>
> **The depths have covered them: they sank into the bottom as a stone.**
>
> **Thy right hand, O LORD, is become glorious in power: thy right hand, O LORD, hath dashed in pieces the enemy [Exod. 15:4–6].**

The Israelites are celebrating their deliverance. Egypt and the Egyptians represent to them the world, slavery, their hopelessness, and helplessness. Now they have been redeemed. That is the sum and substance of their song.

Remember that they have come out of a land of idolatry. Each plague had been leveled at one of the Egyptian gods. Now what is the conclusion they have come to?

> **Who is like unto thee, O LORD, among the gods? who is like thee, glorious in holiness, fearful in praises, doing wonders? [Exod. 15:11].**

God is teaching them great lessons concerning Himself.

> **Thou stretchedst out thy right hand, the earth swallowed them.**
>
> **Thou in thy mercy hast led forth the people which thou hast redeemed: thou hast guided them in thy strength unto thy holy habitation [Exod. 15:12–13].**

Israel was a redeemed people. The redemption of the people had to come first. That is the important thing today. God is not asking you to do one thing for Him until you have been redeemed and have accepted His salvation accomplished by Jesus Christ upon the Cross. He is not asking you for anything. He is not demanding that the world do anything. God is not saying, "If you will prove yourself, come up to a higher standard, wash your face, rake your yard, and put up a good front, I am willing to be your good neighbor." God does not want anything from the world. He is saying to a lost world, "What will you do with My Son who died for you?" Listen once again to verse 13: "Thou in thy mercy hast led forth the people which thou hast redeemed: thou hast guided them in thy strength unto thy holy habitation." It sounds as if they are already in the Promised Land. As far as God is concerned, they are in the land because He is going to take them there.

> **The LORD shall reign for ever and ever.**
>
> **For the horse of Pharaoh went in with his chariots and with his horsemen into the sea, and the LORD brought again the waters of the sea upon them; but the children of Israel went on dry land in the midst of the sea [Exod. 15:18–19].**

Now we are introduced to a girl we have not heard about since the birth of Moses—Miriam, the sister of Moses and Aaron.

> **And Miriam the prophetess, the sister of Aaron, took a timbrel in her hand; and all the women went out after her with timbrels and with dances.**
>
> **And Miriam answered them, Sing ye to the LORD, for he hath triumphed gloriously; the horse and his rider hath he thrown into the sea [Exod. 15:20–21].**

This is the conclusion of this song of praise and thanksgiving to God for His deliverance.

ISRAEL MURMURS BECAUSE THEY LACK WATER

Israel is across the sea now. They have had a wonderful time of praise, singing the song of Moses. They are a redeemed people. You would think that from now on life would be a bed of roses and that they would be delivered from all of their difficulties. There should not have been a cloud in the sky, a thorn along the path, nor a sigh from any of the congregation. They went three days' journey into the wilderness and what happened to them? They thirsted!

> So Moses brought Israel from the Red sea, and they went
> out into the wilderness of Shur; and they went three
> days in the wilderness, and found no water [Exod.
> 15:22].

Egypt had been a land of plenty and with water in abundance. Quite suddenly the children of Israel crossed the Red Sea and found themselves in different circumstances. Water was not available anymore. The cisterns of Egypt were gone and they had not found the fountains of living water. I believe this is the experience of every born-again child of God. After salvation, the believer finds that the cisterns of Egypt do not satisfy at all. There is a period of soul-thirst. This is the period of time Paul speaks of in Philippians 3:7 when he says, "But what things were gain to me, those I counted loss for Christ." Then the apostle Paul reveals a great thirst, a tremendous yearning, when he says in Philippians 3:10, "That I may know him, and the power of his resurrection, and the fellowship of his sufferings, being made conformable unto his death." This is the experience of the child of God after he is redeemed.

I would like to share a personal experience with you. I remember the time God definitely put His hand upon me for the ministry. I came to know the peace of God through trust in Christ. I wanted to study for the ministry, but for the moment I was working in a bank and traveling with a pretty fast crowd. I thought I was having a great time. I was actually the chairman of a dance committee. In those days you always had to have bootleg liquor to dance. I had committed my life to the Lord, but I decided not to break off with the old life all of a sudden. I'd make a gradual break. I decided to go to the dance that night, but I would not dance—just stand in the stag line and visit around a little bit. I was offered a drink at least a dozen times, and each time turned it down. Finally I met a fellow who worked at the bank with me and had a grudge. I was promoted into a position ahead of him, and he had never forgiven me for it. It was not my fault, because I was not in charge of the bank and did not hand out promotions, but he had never forgiven me. He took advantage of every opportunity to get at me in some way, and this evening he said, "This is a pretty place for a preacher to be!" He used some strong language to drive the point home to me, too. I came to the conclusion that what he said was right and, like a little whipped dog, I went down the stairs and out onto the street. I could hear the orchestra playing in the distance, and I almost turned around and went back. I wanted to go back and say to the fellow, "Look, I think I will stay here with the gang." Thank God I did not!

There is always that trip into the wilderness after you are saved. You get a little thirsty, but the cisterns of Egypt just will not satisfy you anymore. You look for living water and actually do not know where to find it. At that time I knew very little about the Bible and couldn't find my way around in it at all. But I soon found John 7:37: "In the last day, that great day of the feast, Jesus stood and cried, saying, If any man thirst, let him come unto me, and drink." What a wonderful thing it was to come to Him!

Thirsting and not finding water was their first experience. Now they have a second experience that was not much better.

And when they came to Marah, they could not drink of the waters of Marah, for they were bitter: therefore the name of it was called Marah.

And the people murmured against Moses, saying, What shall we drink?

And he cried unto the LORD: and the LORD shewed him a tree, which when he had cast into the waters, the waters were made sweet: there he made for them a statute and an ordinance, and there he proved them,

And said, If thou wilt diligently hearken to the voice of the LORD thy God, and wilt do that which is right in his sight, and wilt give ear to his commandments, and keep all his statutes, I will put none of these diseases upon thee, which I have brought upon the Egyptians: for I am the LORD that healeth thee [Exod. 15:23–26].

Their second experience on the other side of the sea is the bitter water of Marah. They have gone three days' journey into the wilderness and are thirsty. When they finally come to water, it is bitter and unfit to drink. And remember that the children of Israel are now redeemed people. Marah was on the path where God led them. He had marked it out for them.

You may not realize it, but the oasis of Marah is a normal Christian experience. When a bitter experience comes to a Christian, it is a puzzling and perplexing thing. Some people say, "Why does God let this happen to me?" I cannot tell you why certain things befall Christians, but I do know that God is not punishing them. He is educating them and preparing them for something. The Lord said, "In the world ye shall have tribulation." Right on your pathway there is a Marah. In the pathway of every believer there is a Marah. God has arranged it all. Someone has said, "Disappointments are God's appointments." I have found this to be true.

Once a young person said to me, "I wanted to go to school. I wanted to prepare for the mission field, but my father died and I had to help support my mother; so I could not go to school." When I was a pastor in Nashville, the superintendent of our junior department was a beautiful, sweet, uncomplaining, young woman. She was prematurely gray, and one day I inquired why. I was told that at one time she was engaged to one of the finest young men in the church. They were to be married, but he was called away to war and was killed. It caused her hair to turn gray. That was the "Marah" in her life.

Friend, there are many frustrations, disappointments, and sorrows in life. Your plans can be torn up like a jigsaw puzzle. You may have a little grave on a hillside somewhere. I have. May I say that we all have our Marahs. You will not bypass them. You cannot detour around them, skip over them, or tunnel under them.

God uses a branding iron. I remember West Texas, in the spring of the year when the calves were branded. As a boy I would see the branding iron put down on a little fellow. Oh, how he bellowed! It made me feel sort of sad to hear him cry. But from then on everyone knew to whom he belonged. After a calf was branded, it would not get lost. God does that for us today.

What was it that made the bitter water of Marah sweet? We are told that a tree cast into the water made it sweet. Deuteronomy 21:23 says, "he that is hanged is accursed of God . . ." and in Galatians 3:13 it says, ". . . Cursed is every one that hangeth on a tree." Jesus Christ died on a tree, and it is that cross that makes the experiences of life sweet. He tasted death for every man, and took the sting out of death. "O death, where is thy sting? O grave, where is thy victory?" says 1 Corinthians 15:55. It is the Cross of Christ that makes sweet the Marah experiences of life.

And they came to Elim, where were twelve wells of water, and threescore and ten palm trees: and they encamped there by the waters [Exod. 15:27].

Elim was a place of abundant blessing and fruitfulness. There were seventy palm trees and twelve wells. After the bitterness of Marah, God brought His people to Elim. "Weeping may endure for a night, but joy cometh in the morning." Simon Peter may be locked in the inner prison, but the angel is going to open the door. Paul and Silas may be beaten at midnight, but an earthquake will free them. There is a Marah along the pilgrim pathway today; but, friend, there is also an Elim. God's plan for usefulness always leads to Marah and to Elim.

Joseph, you remember, had that experience. Moses did, Elijah did, David did, Adoniram Judson did, John G. Paton did. And I am sure you and I will have that also. Beyond every Marah there is an Elim. Beyond every cloud, there is the sun. Beyond every shadow, there is the light. Beyond every trial, there is triumph, and beyond every storm, there is a rainbow. George Matheson wrote, "I trace the rainbow through the rain." This is the way God leads us. All of these things happened to Israel for examples to us.

CHAPTER 16

THEME: Israel murmurs because they lack food; manna and quail are provided by God; manna described and collected; the Sabbath given to Israel

We have been studying the experiences of the nation Israel. After they left the land of Egypt and crossed the Red Sea and came to Mount Sinai, there are seven recorded experiences which correspond to the Christian experience. So far they have sung the song of Moses, gone three days without water, arrived at Marah where the water was bitter, and then journeyed to Elim where there were water and trees in abundance. Elim is a picture of the fruitful Christian experience, and God promises to bring us to this place. Now we come to the Wilderness of Sin, the manna and the quail. And we find that Christ is the Bread of Life.

ISRAEL MURMURS BECAUSE THEY LACK FOOD

And they took their journey from Elim, and all the congregation of the children of Israel came unto the wilderness of Sin, which is between Elim and Sinai, on the fifteenth day of the second month after their departing out of the land of Egypt.

And the whole congregation of the children of Israel murmured against Moses and Aaron in the wilderness:

And the children of Israel said unto them, Would to God we had died by the hand of the LORD in the land of Egypt, when we sat by the flesh pots, and when we did eat bread to the full; for ye have brought us forth into this wilderness, to kill this whole assembly with hunger [Exod. 16:1–3].

It has been only about two and one-half months since the Israelites left Egypt. They started murmuring when they came to the Red Sea. When they crossed the sea, they sang the song of Moses, the song of redemption. But it was not long before they began to murmur again and to sing the Desert Blues. We would call them a bunch of gripers. They wanted to be delivered from the slavery of Egypt, but after they journeyed into the wilderness, they ran short of water and food and began to complain. They remembered the fleshpots of Egypt and longed for them. There are many people who have been saved out of sin, then wanted to go back to the old life. Many of us have had that temptation.

A man told me in Nashville that he was saved out of a life of bootlegging and heavy drinking. When he was converted, he knew every bootlegging joint in Nashville, and for the first few months after he was saved he did not dare go by one of those places because he knew he would go in. He said, "I looked back at those old fleshpots but, thank God, today I hate them."

MANNA AND QUAIL ARE PROVIDED BY GOD

God had no intention of letting His people starve. His plan was to lead them through the wilderness, and He had promised to take care of them.

> Then said the LORD unto Moses, Behold, I will rain bread from heaven for you; and the people shall go out and gather a certain rate every day, that I may prove them, whether they will walk in my law, or no.
>
> And it shall come to pass, that on the sixth day they shall prepare that which they bring in; and it shall be twice as much as they gather daily.
>
> And Moses and Aaron said unto all the children of Israel, At even, then ye shall know that the LORD hath brought you out from the land of Egypt:

> And in the morning, then ye shall see the glory of the
> LORD; for that he heareth your murmurings against the
> LORD: and what are we, that ye murmur against us?
> [Exod. 16:4–7].

Moses and Aaron asked the congregation, "Why are you murmuring against us? We are only human. We cannot do anything. We cannot provide for you. God has heard your murmurings and you will see the glory of God." Every time Israel murmured, the glory of God appeared. This tells us that God does not like griping, complaining, fault-finding Christians. The church is filled with complaining Christians. If you are in a church where you have to murmur, complain, and gripe, get out and go somewhere else.

> And Moses said, This shall be, when the LORD shall give
> you in the evening flesh to eat, and in the morning bread
> to the full; for that the LORD heareth your murmurings
> which ye murmur against him: and what are we? your
> murmurings are not against us, but against the LORD
> [Exod. 16:8].

You should be very careful when you begin to gripe about things at church. Are you griping about the preacher because he is not as friendly as you think he ought to be, or because he did not shake hands with you last Sunday, or because he has not been around to visit you lately? Are you murmuring against him? Aren't you really against him because he teaches the Word of God and represents God in your church? Sometimes we preachers murmur, too, and we all should be careful that we are not murmuring against God. This is one thing that God does not like.

> And Moses spake unto Aaron, Say unto all the congre-
> gation of the children of Israel, Come near before the
> LORD: for he hath heard your murmurings.
>
> And it came to pass, as Aaron spake unto the whole con-
> gregation of the children of Israel, that they looked

toward the wilderness, and, behold, the glory of the
LORD appeared in the cloud.

And the LORD spake unto Moses, saying,

I have heard the murmurings of the children of Israel:
speak unto them, saying, At even ye shall eat flesh, and
in the morning ye shall be filled with bread; and ye
shall know that I am the LORD your God.

And it came to pass, that at even the quails came up,
and covered the camp: and in the morning the dew lay
round about the host [Exod. 16:9–13].

God not only gave the Israelites manna but He sent quail also. They
had quail on toast, or on manna, and it was mighty good eating.

MANNA DESCRIBED AND COLLECTED

Manna was Israel's sustenance as they journeyed through the wilderness.

And when the dew that lay was gone up, behold, upon
the face of the wilderness there lay a small round thing,
as small as the hoar frost on the ground.

And when the children of Israel saw it, they said one to
another, It is manna: for they wist not what it was. And
Moses said unto them, This is the bread which the LORD
hath given you to eat.

This is the thing which the LORD hath commanded,
Gather of it every man according to his eating, an omer
for every man, according to the number of your persons;
take ye every man for them which are in his tents [Exod.
16:14–16].

The Israelites were to gather only enough manna for the day.

> And the children of Israel did so, and gathered, some more, some less.
>
> And when they did mete it with an omer, he that gathered much had nothing over, and he that gathered little had no lack; they gathered every man according to his eating [Exod. 16:17–18].

The glutton did not get more than his share.

> And Moses said, Let no man leave of it till the morning.
>
> Notwithstanding they hearkened not unto Moses; but some of them left of it until the morning, and it bred worms, and stank: and Moses was wroth with them.
>
> And they gathered it every morning, every man according to his eating: and when the sun waxed hot, it melted [Exod. 16:19–21].

The manna was to be gathered every morning. Each man was to gather it. This was to be a personal experience. The manna speaks of the Lord Jesus Christ as the Bread of Life. The Gospel of John, chapter 6, confirms this: "Then Jesus said unto them, Verily, verily, I say unto you, Moses gave you not that bread from heaven; but my Father giveth you the true bread from heaven. For the bread of God is he which cometh down from heaven, and giveth life unto the world. Then said they unto him, Lord, evermore give us this bread. And Jesus said unto them, I am the bread of life: he that cometh to me shall never hunger; and he that believeth on me shall never thirst" (John 6:32–35).

> And it came to pass, that on the sixth day they gathered twice as much bread, two omers for one man: and all the rulers of the congregation came and told Moses.
>
> And he said unto them, This is that which the LORD hath said, To-morrow is the rest of the holy sabbath unto the LORD: bake that which ye will bake to-day, and seethe

that ye will seethe; and that which remaineth over lay up for you to be kept until the morning.

And they laid it up till the morning, as Moses bade: and it did not stink, neither was there any worm therein [Exod. 16:22-24].

God would supply day by day, but before the Sabbath Day they were to get enough for two days.

Manna is that which represents Christ as the Bread of Life who came down from heaven to give His life for the world. Jesus Christ is the true Bread. He is the one who gives us life and sustenance.

In Deuteronomy 8:4 we find that during the forty years that the Israelites wandered in the wilderness their feet did not swell. I have been told by a medical missionary that one of the causes of foot-swelling in the Orient is an improper diet. It is interesting that the manna had all the vitamins they needed to keep their feet from swelling as they journeyed through the wilderness. The manna was adequate to meet their needs.

THE SABBATH GIVEN TO ISRAEL

And Moses said, Eat that to-day; for to-day is a sabbath unto the LORD: to-day ye shall not find it in the field.

Six days ye shall gather it; but on the seventh day, which is the sabbath, in it there shall be none [Exod. 16:25-26].

The Sabbath Day was given to Israel *before* the formal giving of the Law.

And the house of Israel called the name thereof Manna: and it was like coriander seed, white; and the taste of it was like wafers made with honey [Exod. 16:31].

How would you describe manna? It is difficult to explain. It was a wonderful food that contained all the nourishment Israel needed. It tasted, I think, about like anything they wanted it to taste like. It was a very exciting food, but it started the mixed multitude complaining. Numbers 11:4–5 records an incident which helps us to properly understand manna. "And the mixed multitude that was among them fell a-lusting: and the children of Israel also wept again, and said, Who shall give us flesh to eat? We remember the fish, which we did eat in Egypt freely; the cucumbers, and the melons, and the leeks, and the onions, and the garlick." This is what the mixed multitude missed in the wilderness, away from the land of Egypt.

The list of foods that they missed included those which grew on or under the ground. They were condiments without real nourishment like the cucumbers, the melons, the leeks, the onions, and garlic. When you eat some of those things, friends, you are not very attractive. Someone has said, "An apple a day keeps the doctor away." Well, an onion a day keeps everybody away. These are the things that the people of the world eat. They do not satisfy because they are nothing but condiments. The mixed multitude remembered what they had in Egypt and hungered for it.

In Numbers 11:6 it says, "But now our soul is dried away: there is nothing at all, beside this manna, before our eyes." They complained that there was nothing to eat but manna. Numbers 11:7 continues, "And the manna was as coriander seed, and the colour thereof as the colour of bdellium." It is as if God is saying, "These people despise my food which is like fried chicken, ice cream, and angel food cake all rolled into one." Manna was not a monotonous food, but the mixed multitude did not want it.

Numbers 11:8 goes on to say, "And the people went about, and gathered it, and ground it in mills, or beat it in a mortar, and baked it in pans, and made cakes of it: and the taste of it was as the taste of fresh oil." Manna could be fixed in many ways. They could grind it, beat it, bake it in pans, or make a casserole. They probably published *Mother Moses' Cookbook* with 1001 recipes. The children of Israel, however, despised God's heavenly food and complained about eating it. They grew tired of eating manna. They longed for the fleshpots of Egypt. They wanted to go back to that from which they had been delivered.

That is the story, I am afraid, of some people who have been converted, and have been delivered out of "Egypt." Every now and then they take a side trip back to get the leeks, the onions, and the garlic. There are Christians today who need to make a complete break with the old life. Friend, you can't go on living like the world, living on the things of Egypt, and be serviceable to God and have the peace of God in your heart. There must be a break with Egypt. We must live on the true Manna that comes from heaven, even the Lord Jesus Christ.

> **And Moses said, This is the thing which the LORD commandeth, Fill an omer of it to be kept for your generations; that they may see the bread wherewith I have fed you in the wilderness, when I brought you forth from the land of Egypt.**

> **And Moses said unto Aaron, Take a pot, and put an omer full of manna therein, and lay it up before the LORD, to be kept for your generations [Exod. 16:32–33].**

A pot of manna was put in the ark, which is described in greater detail in the final part of Exodus. In the ark were placed three things: (1) Aaron's rod that budded, (2) the pot of manna, and (3) the Ten Commandments. The Law speaks of the fact that Christ alone kept the Law. He fulfilled it for you and me. The manna also speaks of Christ's death for us. He is provided as spiritual food for us. Aaron's rod that budded speaks of His resurrection. Then placed over the ark, serving as the lid, was the mercy seat where the blood was sprinkled. Christ alone was able to meet the demands of God. He alone is able to save, and He can save us because He shed His own blood. Because of that, God can extend mercy to man, the sinner.

> **And the children of Israel did eat manna forty years, until they came to a land inhabited; they did eat manna, until they came unto the borders of the land of Canaan.**

> **Now an omer is the tenth part of an ephah [Exod. 16:35–36].**

These two verses tell us that the children of Israel ate manna for forty years, and we are told what their daily ration was. When they finally came into the Promised Land, the manna ceased, and they ate the old corn of the land again. Then they also complained about the old corn. They discovered that the manna was an exciting food after all. It was, in fact, exotic, compared to the old corn.

The interesting thing about this is that many people live on experience after they have been saved. They have been to the Cross, which speaks of the death of the Lord Jesus Christ, but they go right on talking about their experience. When they give a testimony, they speak only of experience. They do not like Bible study because it is old corn. It is the Word of God that our Lord wants us to feed upon. If you haven't had that taste of manna yet, I suggest that you come to Christ and taste of it. Psalm 34:8 says, "O taste and see that the LORD is good: blessed is the man that trusteth in him." In addition to this, John 6:51 quotes Jesus as saying, "I am the living bread which came down from heaven: if any man eat of this bread, he shall live for ever: and the bread that I will give is my flesh, which I will give for the life of the world."

CHAPTER 17

THEME: *Water flows from the smitten rock; contention with Amalek*

The children of Israel have left the land of Egypt and are on a wilderness march. They are on their way to Mount Sinai. Along the way Israel has had seven experiences that are pictures of the Christian life. Remember, ". . . all these things happened unto them for ensamples: and they are written for our admonition, upon whom the ends of the world are come" (1 Cor. 10:11). All Christians will do well to read and heed these lessons. These lessons are given to us in picture form and their meaning is clear.

WATER FLOWS FROM THE SMITTEN ROCK

As they journey through the desert, the children of Israel thirst and once again they murmur.

> And all the congregation of the children of Israel journeyed from the wilderness of Sin, after their journeys, according to the commandment of the LORD, and pitched in Rephidim: and there was no water for the people to drink.
>
> Wherefore the people did chide with Moses, and said, Give us water that we may drink. And Moses said unto them, Why chide ye with me? wherefore do ye tempt the LORD?
>
> And the people thirsted there for water; and the people murmured against Moses, and said, Wherefore is this that thou hast brought us up out of Egypt, to kill us and our children and our cattle with thirst? [Exod. 17:1–3].

The children of Israel were everlastingly complaining. They have a need and start to complain. God graciously meets their need. Then something else comes up and they begin to cry out, complain, and find fault. Many churches are in this same spiritual condition yet they think they are in excellent condition.

> And Moses cried unto the LORD, saying, What shall I do unto this people? they be almost ready to stone me [Exod. 17:4].

About this time Moses was probably ready to turn his job over to somebody else. Notice God's provision for Israel.

> And the LORD said unto Moses, Go on before the people, and take with thee of the elders of Israel; and thy rod, wherewith thou smotest the river, take in thine hand, and go [Exod. 17:5].

This is the rod given to Moses when he went back to Egypt. It was to be a badge and seal of the authority and power of Moses.

> Behold, I will stand before thee there upon the rock in Horeb; and thou shalt smite the rock, and there shall come water out of it, that the people may drink. And Moses did so in the sight of the elders of Israel.

> And he called the name of the place Massah, and Meribah, because of the chiding of the children of Israel, and because they tempted the LORD, saying, Is the LORD among us, or not? [Exod. 17:6-7].

This is the first mention of the "rock" and the "water" that came out of the rock. What does the rock represent? We are not left to guesswork or our own speculation or our own wisdom. The Holy Spirit of God explains it in 1 Corinthians 10:1-4 which tells us, "Moreover, brethren, I would not that ye should be ignorant, how that all our fathers were under the cloud, and all passed through the sea; and were all baptized unto Moses in the cloud and in the sea; and did all eat the same spiritual meat; and did all drink the same spiritual drink: for they drank of that spiritual Rock that followed them: and that Rock was Christ."

The bread that Israel ate was manna, which was a picture of Christ, the Bread of Life. Christ is also the Water of Life, and the rock is a picture of Him. It contrasts the unbelief of the people (you see, they doubted God here) with the solid rock. Israel was leaning on cobwebs and broken reeds. The small cloud of doubt was hiding the face of God from them.

The rock is a beautiful portrait of the Lord Jesus Christ. Psalm 61:2 says, "From the end of the earth will I cry unto thee, when my heart is overwhelmed: lead me to the rock that is higher than I." That is Christ. Again the psalmist says, "And they remembered that God was their rock, and the high God their redeemer" (Ps. 78:35). Then Peter tells us, "Wherefore also it is contained in the scripture, Behold, I lay in Sion a chief corner stone, elect, precious: and he that believeth on him shall not be confounded. Unto you therefore which believe he is precious: but unto them which be disobedient, the stone which the builders disallowed, the same is made the head of the corner, And a stone of stumbling, and a rock of offence, even to them which stumble at the word, being disobedient: whereunto also they were appointed" (1 Pet. 2:6–8). Finally, the apostle Paul gives us this advice in 1 Corinthians 3:11, "For other foundation can no man lay than that is laid, which is Jesus Christ."

The Lord Jesus, as one hymn says, is "a Rock in a weary land." Although this is a marvelous picture of Him as the foundation—the One upon whom we rest and the One upon whom the church is built—a rock is the last place we go for a drink of water. I do not mean to be facetious, but you could not even get hard water from a rock. That would be like getting blood from a turnip or orange juice from a doorknob. You can admire a rock's sterling qualities and durability. There are great lessons to be learned from it. You can test it and analyze it, but you cannot drink it. Jesus is a Rock, but His beautiful life and durability will not save you. His teachings will not redeem your soul. His life and teachings are like polished marble which are engraved and, though you apply them to your life with Carborundum or optician's rouge, they still won't save you. The application of the principles taught by the Lord Jesus may polish you a little, but He is still the Rock against which you can dash your foot.

You can fall on the Rock, Christ Jesus, for salvation, but no human effort is able to get water from this Rock. Only when the rock was smitten did it bring forth life-giving waters. Jesus was crucified, and nothing short of believing that He died in your place and bore your sins on that Cross will save you. The smitten rock is a picture of the death of Jesus Christ.

In Numbers we are told a second time that the children of Israel complained that they had no water. The first time Israel murmured about being thirsty God told Moses to strike the rock and water gushed forth. In Numbers, however, God gives Moses different instructions. God tells Moses: "Take the rod, and gather thou the assembly together, thou, and Aaron thy brother, and *speak ye unto the rock* before their eyes; and it shall give forth his water, and thou shalt bring forth to them water out of the rock: so thou shalt give the congregation and their beasts drink" (Num. 20:8). Moses was to *speak* to the rock because the rock had already been *smitten*. Christ was crucified nineteen hundred years ago, and when He said on the Cross, "It is finished. . ." (John 19:30), it was indeed finished. Christ does not have to be crucified again. God is satisfied with what Jesus did for you. The question is, "Are you satisfied with the work Christ did for you on the Cross?" He died to save you. All that God is asking is that you believe in His Son.

From the Rock, Christ Jesus, come spiritual blessings today. The waters of blessing gush forth to relieve parched lips. Ephesians 1:3 informs us that, "Blessed be the God and Father of our Lord Jesus Christ, who hath blessed us with all spiritual blessings in heavenly places in Christ." The Rock was smitten *once* and from it flows an abundance of water. The fountain is brim full. The stream is bank full. The world is not able to contain it. But in spite of that, there are many men's souls that are shriveled up and tongues that are parched. Millions of people are dying for want of spiritual drink. The channel is blocked, log-jammed by doubts, corroded by sin, and insulated by indifference. The channel is also dammed by those who profess to know Jesus Christ but who in reality do not know Him.

Friends, I am disturbed and distressed as I look about. The world is thirsty. I ask you personally and particularly, Have you been to that smitten Rock for a drink of living water? God says if you drink of that water you will never thirst again.

CONTENTION WITH AMALEK

During their wilderness march the Israelites ran into the Amalekites, who represent the flesh in Scripture. This experience is yet another lesson we would do well to learn.

> **Then came Amalek, and fought with Israel in Rephidim [Exod. 17:8].**

Amalek was a descendant of Esau, and the Amalekites had become enemies of Israel. They never ceased to be Israel's enemies. For the first time the children of Israel engage in warfare.

> **And Moses said unto Joshua, Choose us out men, and go out, fight with Amalek: to-morrow I will stand on the top of the hill with the rod of God in mine hand.**
>
> **So Joshua did as Moses had said to him, and fought with Amalek: and Moses, Aaron, and Hur went up to the top of the hill [Exod. 17:9–10].**

Esau was a picture of the flesh. As Israel could not overcome Amalek by their own efforts, neither can you nor I overcome the flesh by our own efforts. The flesh wars against the spirit and the spirit against the flesh. Paul explains it in Galatians 5:17, "For the flesh lusteth against the Spirit, and the Spirit against the flesh: and these are contrary the one to the other: so that ye cannot do the things that ye would." This is the picture we have in the wilderness as Israel and Amalek war against each other.

> And it came to pass, when Moses held up his hand, that
> Israel prevailed: and when he let down his hand, Ama-
> lek prevailed.
>
> But Moses' hands were heavy; and they took a stone,
> and put it under him, and he sat thereon; and Aaron
> and Hur stayed up his hands, the one on the one
> side, and the other on the other side; and his hands
> were steady until the going down of the sun [Exod.
> 17:11–12].

Careful observation reveals that the battle was actually fought on top of the mountain. It was fought by prayer. This battle was not won by Israel's fighting ability because they were not experienced soldiers nor adept at warfare yet. This battle was fought and won by Moses. The moment Moses was no longer able to hold his hands up, the children of Israel began to lose the fight. If it had not been for Moses, Israel would have lost the battle. The important thing to remember is that the Holy Spirit is the only One who can give us victory over the flesh. Victory comes as the believer walks in the Spirit. When you and I act independently of the Spirit, Amalek, or the flesh, wins an easy victory. When Moses' hands were held up, the Israelites won. You and I never will be able to overcome the flesh. It is only the Spirit of God who can do that.

> And Joshua discomfited Amalek and his people with
> the edge of the sword.
>
> And the LORD said unto Moses, Write this for a memorial
> in a book, and rehearse it in the ears of Joshua: for I will
> utterly put out the remembrance of Amalek from under
> heaven [Exod. 17:13–14].

It is time to stop and consider this man Joshua. He is the one who is going to succeed Moses. We can see that he is already being prepared for this position. He is an ordinary man but God is preparing him for the task that is ahead of him. God instructs Moses to rehearse in the ears of Joshua that Amalek is to be destroyed.

Now God is going to get rid of the flesh. Thank God for that. When the Lord takes the church to heaven, He will change it. 1 Corinthians 15:52 confirms this: "In a moment, in the twinkling of an eye, at the last trump: for the trumpet shall sound, and the dead shall be raised incorruptible, and we shall be changed." If the Lord took the church to heaven as it is now, without changing it, heaven would be just like this old earth because we would wreck the place with our old natures. I have been dragging my old nature around like a corpse for years. I would like to get rid of it, and I have tried to get rid of it, but it keeps asserting itself again and again. Thank God that He has promised to get rid of Vernon McGee's old nature one day. Those who belong to Christ will some day be changed and made fit for heaven.

> **And Moses built an altar, and called the name of it Jehovah-nissi:**
>
> **For he said, Because the LORD hath sworn that the LORD will have war with Amalek from generation to generation [Exod. 17:15–16].**

There are three important things to remember. First, God is going to get rid of Amalek. In other words, God is going to get rid of the old nature. Secondly, the Lord will never compromise with the old nature. He will have war with Amalek from generation to generation. The third important item is that this constant conflict will go on as long as we live in this life. The flesh and the spirit will always war against each other. Only the Holy Spirit of God can give us victory. We need to recognize this fact.

CHAPTER 18

THEME: The visit of Jethro, Moses' father-in-law;
Jethro's advice to appoint judges accepted by Moses

In chapter 18 we come to the last of the seven experiences the children of Israel had between Egypt and Mount Sinai. God has been leading Moses directly by revelation but now Moses turns to worldly wisdom for help rather than to God for revelation.

THE VISIT OF JETHRO, MOSES' FATHER-IN-LAW

Jethro, the priest of Midian, visits Moses. He brought Moses' wife and children with him. While with Moses, they have a nice visit; you might call it a family reunion.

> When Jethro, the priest of Midian, Moses' father-in-law, heard of all that God had done for Moses, and for Israel his people, and that the LORD had brought Israel out of Egypt;
>
> Then Jethro, Moses' father-in-law, took Zipporah, Moses' wife, after he had sent her back,
>
> And her two sons; of which the name of the one was Gershom; for he said, I have been an alien in a strange land:
>
> And the name of the other was Eliezer; for the God of my father, said he, was mine help, and delivered me from the sword of Pharaoh [Exod. 18:1–4].

Moses has come now into the land of Midian with this great company of Israelites. Here the father-in-law of Moses brings his wife and sons to him. Apparently, when they went down to Egypt, after that experience when she called him a bloody husband, he sent her back home—

then or shortly after that. There is no record of her being in Egypt when the Exodus took place. But now Jethro brings her and her two sons to Moses. So this is a family reunion.

> And Jethro, Moses' father-in-law, came with his sons and his wife unto Moses into the wilderness, where he encamped at the mount of God:
>
> And he said unto Moses, I thy father-in-law Jethro am come unto thee, and thy wife, and her two sons with her.
>
> And Moses went out to meet his father-in-law, and did obeisance, and kissed him; and they asked each other of their welfare; and they came into the tent [Exod. 18:5–7].

It is an interesting thing to note the marvelous relationship between Moses and his father-in-law. They seem to be very close, buddies in fact. Moses tells him all that God has done in leading the children of Israel out of Egypt. Jethro shows great interest in everything that Moses relates to him. In fact, when Moses went out to greet his family, we are told that he kissed his father-in-law but nothing is said about him kissing his wife. This passage says nothing about Moses being glad to see his sons either. All of this seems to confirm our previous conclusion that Moses' family relationship was not as it should have been.

> And Moses told his father-in-law all that the LORD had done unto Pharaoh and to the Egyptians for Israel's sake, and all the travail that had come upon them by the way, and how the LORD delivered them.
>
> And Jethro rejoiced for all the goodness which the LORD had done to Israel, whom he had delivered out of the hand of the Egyptians.
>
> And Jethro said, Blessed be the LORD, who hath delivered you out of the hand of the Egyptians, and out of the

hand of Pharaoh, who hath delivered the people from under the hand of the Egyptians.

Now I know that the LORD is greater than all gods: for in the thing wherein they dealt proudly he was above them.

And Jethro, Moses' father-in-law, took a burnt offering and sacrifices for God: and Aaron came, and all the elders of Israel, to eat bread with Moses' father-in-law before God [Exod. 18:8–12].

Jethro was probably skeptical when Moses, while still in Midian, announced that he was going to deliver the children of Israel from their yoke of bondage in Egypt. Probably he told his neighbors, "I don't know what has come over my son-in-law. He has big ideas. He thinks God has called him to deliver the Israelites out of Egypt. I just don't believe that the God he serves can do that." Well, God did do it, and this apparently brought Jethro to a saving knowledge of God. This is evidenced by the fact that he offered burnt offerings to God.

JETHRO'S ADVICE TO APPOINT JUDGES ACCEPTED BY MOSES

And it came to pass on the morrow, that Moses sat to judge the people: and the people stood by Moses from the morning unto the evening.

And when Moses' father-in-law saw all that he did to the people, he said, What is this thing that thou doest to the people? why sittest thou thyself alone, and all the people stand by thee from morning unto even?

And Moses said unto his father-in-law, Because the people come unto me to inquire of God:

When they have a matter, they come unto me; and I judge between one and another, and I do make them know the statutes of God, and his laws.

And Moses' father-in-law said unto him, The thing that
thou doest is not good.

Thou wilt surely wear away, both thou, and this people
that is with thee: for this thing is too heavy for thee; thou
art not able to perform it thyself alone [Exod. 18:13–18].

Moses' father-in-law obviously loved him, had great respect for him,
and was enthusiastic about him. As he has brought Moses' family to
be with him, he stays on for a few days and sees how busy Moses is,
judging the people. So he comes up with a suggestion to lighten the
load of Moses.

Hearken now unto my voice, I will give thee counsel,
and God shall be with thee: Be thou for the people to
God-ward, that thou mayest bring the causes unto God:

And thou shalt teach them ordinances and laws, and
shalt shew them the way wherein they must walk, and
the work that they must do.

Moreover thou shalt provide out of all the people able
men, such as fear God, men of truth, hating covetous-
ness; and place such over them, to be rulers of thousands, and rulers of hundreds, rulers of fifties, and
rulers of tens:

And let them judge the people at all seasons: and it shall
be, that every great matter they shall bring unto thee,
but every small matter they shall judge: so shall it be
easier for thyself, and they shall bear the burden with
thee.

If thou shalt do this thing, and God command thee so,
then thou shalt be able to endure, and all this people
shall also go to their place in peace.

So Moses hearkened to the voice of his father-in-law,
and did all that he had said.

> And Moses chose able men out of all Israel, and made
> them heads over the people, rulers of thousands, rulers
> of hundreds, rulers of fifties, and rulers of tens.
>
> And they judged the people at all seasons: the hard
> causes they brought unto Moses, but every small matter
> they judged themselves.
>
> And Moses let his father-in-law depart; and he went his
> way into his own land [Exod. 18:19–27].

Jethro suggested that judges be appointed to help Moses take care of the problems of the people. Someone is apt to say, "What is wrong with his suggestion?" Well, on the surface, everything looks fine.

One thing must be remembered—there are two kinds of wisdom in this world, the wisdom of God and the wisdom of this world. Jethro's proposal was based on the wisdom of the world. When you follow the pattern of the world, you do not look to God. One of the reasons the church is in such trouble today is because men have been brought into the church and put on a board or given a place of prominence because they have been successful in business. They attempt to run the church by the methods of the world, and they have no spiritual discernment whatsoever. The program of the world does not work in the church.

The recommendations that Jethro made were good. They would take the load off Moses and expedite matters. They would provide an orderly system and conserve time. Jethro's proposition looked like a very attractive package. His suggestion was sincere, and he meant well. He was concerned about Moses' health, and you cannot help but love him for this. The thing, however, that we need to note is that it was not the will of God. God permitted it all right, but He did not suggest it.

A careful examination of this passage will reveal the subtle and sinister character of this man's advice. First of all, God had given no such instructions to Moses concerning this matter. Jethro's suggestion actually questioned the wisdom, judgment, and the love of God. Jethro was actually saying that God was not doing the best that He could for Moses. If God really loved Moses and cared for him, He would have made this suggestion a long time ago. Friends, I hear in back of Jethro's statement the hiss of the serpent made known so long ago in the Garden of Eden. The serpent had suggested to Eve, "Oh, if you could only eat of that tree, you would be wise and God has not permitted you to do that. God is not doing the best that He could do for you." Jethro's suggestion implies the same thing. But if this were the best method, God would have made this arrangement before.

The second thing to note is that God had been dealing directly with Moses. He was equipping him for the great task of delivering Israel. God did not want a third party brought in. He did not want others included who would dissipate or insulate the power of God in coming directly to Moses. Remember that God spoke face-to-face with Moses. There are many people who do not like to do business directly with God. They would rather deal with other people. They would rather go through a man, a church, a ceremony, a book, or even go to a musical concert. All of these have their place. But, friend, we need to go directly to God. God didn't want this crowd brought into it.

The third thing to notice, as we look at this passage, is that Jethro's suggestion created an organization out of which came the seventy, the Sanhedrin, which one night about 1500 years after this met together and plotted the death of the Son of God! Moses didn't need this organization. God gave Moses power for the task and these arduous duties. These seventy men were no more efficient for God than one man. After all, it is the Spirit that quickeneth and gives man power.

There are people who feel that what the church needs for success is the right method. Right now there are many preachers who are acting rather foolishly by trying to identify themselves with the "new generation." They say that they want to communicate with the new generation. There is a seminary in Southern California that majors in identifying and communicating with people. I have never heard of them really reaching down and touching lives in Southern California. They just cannot do it. God does not need a method, an organization, numbers, a system, a ritual, or good works. God sweeps aside all the wisdom of the world so that there is nothing between your soul and Him. The wisdom of the world and the wisdom of God are contradictory—so much so that one is wisdom and the other is foolishness. In 1 Corinthians 3:18–19 God says, "Let no man deceive himself. If any man among you seemeth to be wise in this world, let him become a fool, that he may be wise. For the wisdom of this world is foolishness with God. For it is written, He taketh the wise in their own craftiness."

The apostle Paul tells us in 1 Corinthians 2:4, ". . . my speech and my preaching was not with enticing words of man's wisdom, but in demonstration of the Spirit and of power." We do not need to be clever and use the intellectual approach to win men to Christ. What we do need is the wisdom of God to guide us. We need the power of God and not new methods. My friend, do you rely on the wisdom of the world or do you look to God to guide you with that wisdom that is from above?

BIBLIOGRAPHY
(Recommended for Further Study)

Borland, James A. *Christ in the Old Testament.* Chicago, Illinois: Moody Press, 1978.

Davis, John J. *Moses and the Gods of Egypt.* Grand Rapids, Michigan: Baker Book House, 1971.

Epp, Theodore H. *Moses.* Lincoln, Nebraska: Back to the Bible Broadcast, 1975.

Gaebelein, Arno C. *Annotated Bible.* Vol. I. Neptune, New Jersey: Loizeaux Brothers, 1917.

Gispen, William Hendrik. *Exodus.* Grand Rapids, Michigan: Zondervan Publishing House, 1982.

Grant, F. W. *Numerical Bible.* Neptune, New Jersey: Loizeaux Brothers, 1891.

Gray, James M. *Synthetic Bible Studies.* Old Tappan, New Jersey: Fleming H. Revell Company, 1906.

Huey, F. B., Jr. *Exodus: Bible Study Commentary.* Grand Rapids, Michigan: Zondervan Publishing House, 1977.

Jensen, Irving L. *Exodus.* Chicago, Illinois: Moody Press, 1967.

Mackintosh, C. H. (C.H.M.). *Notes on the Pentateuch.* Neptune, New Jersey: Loizeaux Brothers, 1880.

McGee, J. Vernon. *The Tabernacle, God's Portrait of Christ.* Pasadena, California: Thru the Bible Books.

Meyer, F. B. *Exodus.* Grand Rapids, Michigan: Kregel Publications, 1952.

Meyer, F. B. *Moses: The Servant of God.* Fort Washington, Pennsylvania: Christian Literature Crusade, n.d.

Morgan, G. Campbell. *The Unfolding Message of the Bible.* Old Tappan, New Jersey: Fleming H. Revell Company.

Pink, Arthur W. *Gleanings in Exodus.* Chicago, Illinois: Moody Press, 1922.

Ridout, Samuel. *Lectures on the Tabernacle.* Neptune, New Jersey: Loizeaux Brothers, 1914.

Thomas W. H. Griffith. *Through the Pentateuch Chapter by Chapter.* Grand Rapids, Michigan: William B. Eerdmans Company, 1957.

Unger, Merrill F. *Unger's Bible Handbook.* Chicago, Illinois: Moody Press, 1966.

Unger, Merrill F. *Unger's Commentary on the Old Testament*, Vol. I. Chicago, Illinois: Moody Press, 1981.

Youngblood, Ronald F. *Exodus.* Chicago, Illinois: Moody Press, 1983.